THE ARTISANS IN 18th CENTURY EASTERN INDIA

About the Author

Vipul Singh (*b.* 1969) is Lecturer of Medieval History at Motilal Nehru College, (University of Delhi), New Delhi, where he has been teaching since 1998. He obtained his M.A., M.Phil and Ph.D in History from Delhi University.

Dr. Singh specialises on eighteenth century Indian history which is considered as a period of transition from medieval to modern. He has to his credit a number of research papers, articles and book-reviews, published in journals of repute. He has participated in many national and international conferences.

Among his publications, the chapter entitled "Ecology and Encounters : The Maratha Demands and its Impact on Land-use Pattern in Eighteenth Century Marwar" published in the book *Resource Conservation and Food Security*, (Concept Publishing Company, New Delhi, 2004) has been widely acclaimed for its meticulous research. Presently, Dr. Singh is engaged in writing a volume on the environmental history of Marwar.

THE ARTISANS IN 18th CENTURY EASTERN INDIA

A History of Survival

by
Vipul Singh

CONCEPT PUBLISHING COMPANY, NEW DELHI-110059

Cataloging in Publication Data—DK
Courtesy: D.K. Agencies (P) Ltd. <docinfo@dkagencies.com>

Singh, Vipul, 1969-
The artisans in 18th century eastern India : a history of survival / by Vipul Singh.
p. cm.
Includes bibliographical references (p.)
Includes index.
ISBN 8180692353

1. Artisans—India—Patna (District)—Social conditions—18th century.
2. Artisans—India—Patna (Diastrict)—Economic conditions—18th century.
I. Title. II. Title: Artisans in eighteenth century eastern India.

DDC 331.794 095 412 21

ISBN : 81-8069-235-3

First Published 2005

Published and Printed by
Ashok Kumar Mittal
Concept Publishing Company
A/15-16, Commercial Block, Mohan Garden
New Delhi-110059 (India)

Phones : 25351460, 25351794
Fax : 091-11-25357103
Email : publishing@conceptpub.com

Dedicated to
those who do not study
but create history and whose
history is rarely mentioned
in historical texts

PREFACE

This work has been in the offing for a long time. My fieldwork and research on this subject began in 1994 with the funding of Indian Council of Historical Research (ICHR), New Delhi, continuing till 1996 as part of M. Phil thesis. However, I could not get down to the work of writing a book in real earnest till I had finished my another research project for Ph.D. degree again on the eighteenth century, but on a different Indian region. In between I managed to publish few articles in different journals of repute and got the feedback from various quarters. Then I decided to revise my M.Phil thesis and a manuscript for this was prepared by incorporating relevant literatures published since 1996.

Eighteenth century is a period sandwitched between two major empires—the Mughal and the British and therefore, historical research has created ripples and debates of two divergent expositions called 'continuity' and 'change'. The present book challenges many cherished notions of prosperity in the second half of the eighteenth century. In response to the 'continuity' thesis, the book views the colonial state as being located externally to the Indian society and sees colonialism economically exploitative in nature and substance.

The central theme of the book is the socio-economic condition of the artisans and their survival in the wake of the colonial onslaught in the eastern part of India i.e. Patna during the second half of the eighteenth century. The primary documents used for this volume are *Francis Buchanan's Account of Patna District, Fort-William India House Correspondence and* two untapped vernacular literatures—*Naqsh-e-Paidar* and *Yadgar-e-Rozgar.*

Researching for and writing my thesis and more recently this book, lead to deep obligations and debt to many people who encouraged and assisted in one way or another.

The present book would hardly have been possible without the friendly prompting and personal interest of Shri Ashok Kumar Mittal, Concept Publishing Company, New Delhi.

I would like to gratefully acknowledge the sympathy and consideration shown to me by Prof. Dilbagh Singh, Prof. B.P. Sahu, Prof. T.K. Venkat Subramanian, Prof. R.L. Shukla, Dr. R.P. Rana, and Dr. M.L. Bhatia.

I am specially thankful to Dr. V.K. Jain and Dr. R.P. Bahuguna, once my teachers and now colleagues, for their thoughtful suggestions. Dr. Divik Ramesh, Sh. S.C. Chibber, Dr. S.B. Bharadwaj, Dr. Surendra Sahai, Sh. Pawan Sinha and Sh. Netrapal Singh at Motilal Nehru College always encouraged for the completion of the book.

My didi Dr. Ruby Roy, Fellow at Institute for Defence Studies and Analyses, and Dr. Tapeshwar Singh, Associate Professor at M.M.H. College Ghaziabad, have been an uninterrupted source of inspiration for me.

I was also helped and encouraged by my colleagues and friends at Delhi University and elsewhere. Mrs. Kavita Asthana was generous with time and effort when she painstakingly went through the final proof.

Thanks are also due to the staff of Central Reference Library, Delhi University; Nehru Memorial Library, New Delhi; ICHR Library, New Delhi; National Archives of India, New Delhi; Khuda Baksh Oriental Public Library, Patna; Sinha Library, Patna and A.N. Sinha Institute Library, Patna.

I am also obliged to my wife Mrs. Neelam Singh, who has taken time off her own teaching work in preparing the maps with her expertise on cartography. Varnika and Yug have innocently inspired me to complete the work. And finally I owe debt to my father Sh. Birendra Pratap Singh and Maa for providing me with inspiration and necessary strength.

Vipul Singh

CONTENTS

ABBREVIATIONS

Buchanan	:	An Account of Districts of Bihar and Patna in 1811-12.
CEHI	:	The Cambridge Economic History of India.
CHB	:	The Comprehensive History of Bihar.
CPC	:	Calendar of Persian Correspondence (National Archives of India, New Delhi).
FWC	:	Fort William-India House Correspondence. (National Archives of India, New Delhi).
IESHR	:	Indian Economic and Social History Review.
JBORS	:	Journal of Bihar and Orissa Research Society.
JIH	:	Journal of Indian History.
PIHC	:	Proceedings of Indian History Congress.

INTRODUCTION

Over the last few decades the scholars researching on the eighteenth century Indian history have not been able to distance themselves from ongoing debate on the nature of the eighteenth century. There is no denying the fact that no one pattern of change characterizes the century and different regions followed their own trajectories of development, but some general features are certainly discernible across the country, specially in the wake of the beginning of the colonial rule.

The eighteenth century is featured with two critical transitions, which changed the structure of power and initiated important social and economic refigurations-the Mughal decline in the first half and political and economic prominence of the East India Company in the second half. Therefore, studies on the first half of the eighteenth century have their own line of arguments on the nature of economic and social change in the wake of imperial collapse and have led researchers to take either of the two divergent positions of 'Dark age'[1]—meaning political, economic and social breakdown—and 'economic prosperity'[2]—meaning political and economic reconfigurations by regional powers. The debate on the second half of the eighteenth century centres around the implications of transition in society and economy with the political supremacy of the English East India Company. One set of positions views the colonial rule as determining economic as well as political disjunction, indicating 'change'.[3] This view is contested by the argument that the East India Company was sucked into the vibrant indigenous political economies and continued many of the regional economic and cultural referents meaning 'continuity'[4] of the earlier period. The proponents of this continuity thesis argue that the disintegration of the Mughal empire didnot produce destabilizing effects on country's trade and commerce and the artisans. On the contrary, it generated forces of regeneration and growth throughout India. The continuity in the economic development was thus maintained without being interrupted by the establishment of British imperial power in later half of the eighteenth century. But the moot point to understand here is that the East India Company took advantage of the absence of strong opposition to step into it, and therefore, it was bound to have serious implications on polity, society and economy.

The present study of an important region-Patna, located in the eastern part of India in eighteenth century Bengal, tries to highlight the centrality of the region in European export trade in textiles, silk, and other items leading to prosperity of artisans well upto 1765 before the East India Company got the *diwani* of Bengal. But the gradual intervention and take over by the company rule, the artisans in particular had to suffer tremendously. We have tried to trace the history of survival of the artisans in the wake of colonial onslaught. The focus is on the socio-economic affairs of the artisans and their industries, tracing the gradual demise of their economic status and their resistance to formidable European companies like the Dutch East India Company and the English East India Company.

In recent times socio-economic history has attracted a good deal of attention. Few good studies have been done relating to the class of the artisans and the non-agrarian production in north India as well as for the south India.[5] They offer us a good framework for undertaking detailed studies at the micro-level.

The period we are taking up for study is between AD 1765 and 1811 regarding the artisans residing in Patna district. The importance of the period lies in the fact that this period acted as a transitional phase for Eastern India including Patna district. The economic impact of British rule was being increasingly felt. The authority of the Mughal empire had long been declining and this process of decline was precipitated with the establishment of the British administrative system after the battle of Buxar and specially after the grant of *diwani* of Bengal to the East India Company in 1765. The year 1811 is significant in the sense that in this year Francis Buchanan[6] undertook the massive exercise to survey this region in order to make the British policy-framers better informed about the administrative structure and the state of economy and society, so that they could formulate their policy accordingly.

The secondary work on Patna region for the above mentioned period is an edited work, *The Comprehensive History of Bihar*[7] by K.K. Datta. It contains a detailed account of the history of Bihar from middle of the eighteenth century onwards. It is a narrative of the advent and early activities of the European trading companies in Bihar. The sites of their factories and the principal items of their trade like cotton cloth, saltpetre among many others, and their relation with the local government have also been discussed.

Hameeda Khatoon Naqvi in her book *Urban Centres and Industries in Upper India (1556-1803)*[8], has done extensive researches on various urban centres and industries from Lahore to Patna between 1556 and 1803. She opines that the grant of *diwani* entitled the British to political domination and enabled them to exercise stringent control over their production, sale and export.

Other works of significance which confine the focus of their study to Patna and the adjoining regions are, *Bihar Through the Ages*[9] by R.R. Diwakar, *Patna in the Nineteenth Century*[10] by Surendra Gopal, and *Patna Through the Ages*[11] edited by Qeyamuddin Ahmad. Diwakar's book deals with the history of Bihar right from ancient to modern times. Apart from resorting to wide generalisations, it concentrates mainly on political history of Patna. Though there are few passing references to the craft industries located in Patna, but that is only with reference to trade and commerce. Surendra Gopal and Ranjan Sinha[12] too have emphasized on the trading and commercial importance of Patna and the persistent rivalry among various European companies to dominate the scene.

In order to study the artisans of Patna district we have attempted a comprehensive analysis of this class during the second half of the eighteenth and early nineteenth century. The book has been divided into six chapters. The first chapter deals with the historical geography of Patna district, which has been further sub-divided into three parts consisting of physical geography, administrative history of the region and the symbiosis of European powers. The motives of the British administrators behind the formation of Patna district and the competition among various European companies have been studied. Some questions are also raised to examine whether it was done only by a readjustment of the earlier *pargana* divisions or any new *pargana* was also created? We have also examined whether the district boundary was fixed on the geofiscal basis or it was just an administrative division for convenience to rule effectively. An 'appendix' *(Clive's letter to the Court of Directors,* Calcutta, 30th September 1765) on the British motive behind the acquisition of the *Diwani* rights of Bihar, Bengal and Orissa has been put up at the end of the book to highlight the administrative measures.

Chapter two and three deal with Artisans' craftsmanship and the organisation of production. In the course of discussion under this head we have taken up certain pertinent questions such as — who constituted the artisan class? Whether the artisans were mainly involved in traditional industries? What were the traditional methods of production in various industries followed by the local artisans? Which were the production centres? Was there mobility among the artisans? This will also include the discussion on caste-dynamics of the artisans. What types of technological innovations were made in the performance of age old traditional industries? The chapter on organisation of production includes the applicability of *Karkhana* system and putting out system if at all in the system of manufacturing. Further, what was the nature of earnings of the artisans i.e. whether they were wage-earners or owned their own small household units, has also been discussed.

Chapter four discusses the trading activities of the European companies and local traders. It tries to show that how the regional trade of the local traders remained confined to items of local consumption, and it is the European traders who began dominating the trade of more profitable items like saltpetre and textile.

The fifth chapter concentrates on the impact of colonisation on crafts and craftsmen. How the condition of artisans deteriorated under the colonial policy of monopolisation of production is the main emphasis here. We have also analysed the viewpoints of various historians around the issue of deindustrialisation taking Patna district as a case study. Chapter six gives the conclusive analysis on the survival of the artisans. There are three appendices at the end of the book. The first one is Clive's letter to the court of directors and the second gives the list of ninety-five types of artisans and their population in Patna district. The third appendix is regarding a series of regulations imposed on weavers during the last decades of the eighteenth century.

The main source we have used here is Buchanan's Report on various districts of Bihar, specially Patna. We have used this source mainly because we are not in access of any other contemporary indigenous work on Patna district. Buchanan surveyed a number of districts like Patna, Bhagalpur, Purnea, etc. during the first and second decades of the nineteenth century under the order of the East India Company. He was given the task of recording the population, agricultural and mineral resources giving details of flora and fauna, the means of livelihood of the people, the land tenure systems and the history of these regions. He collected massive information in his survey reports. His methods of collection of data were apparently very thorough and detailed. He covered most of the area by road, halting at the important marts and towns, and keeping notes all the while.[13] In this cumbersome process he was assisted by the local officials since he was an authorised agent of the East India Company. Besides he was accompanied by his own assistants who acted as interpreters and recorded the information.

Apart from keeping official records, Buchanan also maintained elaborate Journals of his travels.[14] These Journals... "are of the nature of official diaries kept by Buchanan, recording his movements from day to day, with the distance travelled, the features of the country passed through the sites and objects of interest examined, the inquiries made on subjects of archaeological, historical, ethnological, geological etc. interest... The statistical information collected e.g. as to population, castes, professions, number of towns and villages, education, soils and methods of cultivation, livestock, manufacturers, exports and imports etc., all of which are dealt with at length in the Reports and Appendices thereto... All this information was recorded by his Indian assistants; while the drawings and copies of inscriptions etc. were made by a draftsman who accompanied him."[15]

It is the enormous amount of information provided by Buchanan which has helped us to carry out the present research. His survey was thorough enough for those days that all economic historians after him have used his data as bench-marks e.g. W. Hunter in his *Statistical Accounts of Bengal* has time and again compared the current data with those of Buchanan.[16]

Due to a long and continuous stay of English factors at Patna, a whole series of official correspondence was done from here. Their correspondences and letters are very useful for our purpose, which are available to us in edited and sometimes in original. *Fort William - India House Correspondence,*[17] *Patna Commissioner's Record*[18], are few of the many such records which provide information regarding the state of things prevailing during the second half of the eighteenth century and the changes that occurred in administrative set-up. *Fort William - India House Correspondences* give a clear picture of the policy of the British which they followed and with what motive. Why did they really bothered to settle a Cantonment around Patna and the district as such, are mentioned in these official letters. They also give us information on relations of the British East India Company with other European powers and its policy to monopolise the production as well as trade in Patna district.

Patna Commissioner's Record provides us with the factual information on the creation of Patna as a separate judicial district. The letters from Commissioners of Patna also report on the separation of Patna Collectorship from Behar Collectorship and areas included in Patna district.

Apart from these British sources, we are in access of two local literary texts in Urdu - *Naqsh-e-Paidar*[19] and *Yadgar-e-Rozgar.*[20] Although they are of the later period and not extensive enough on arts and crafts so as to do a holistic research, they are useful for supplementing the evidences on Patna district. Both these works are full of praise for the local arts and crafts. The authors of these works see how the production in foreign hands had placed the Indian handicrafts in an unfavourable situation, how the fiscal policies of the government, particularly discriminatory taxation and tariff policies, adversely affected local industries and crafts. They also draw attention to the need to patronize local handicrafts and suggest that indigenously produced articles should be purchased even at a higher price not only for their intrinsic merit or quality but also to support the large number of persons who earn their livelihood through these crafts.

NOTES

1. Irfan Habib, Athar Ali and Satish Chandra are the main proponents of the 'Dark Age' theory. See Irfan Habib, 'Eighteenth Century in Indian Economic History', *Proceedings of the Indian History Congress,* 56th session, Calcutta, 1995, pp. 358-78. M. Athar Ali, 'The Eighteenth Century : An Interpretation', *Indian Historical Review,* 5 (1-2), 1978-9, pp. 175-86. Satish Chandra, 'Review of the Crisis of the Jagirdari System', in Satish Chandra, *Medieval India : Society, the Jagirdari Crisis, and the Village,* Delhi, 1982.
2. The proponents of 'Economic Prosperity' theory see the political change as a result of Mughal decline not as a crisis, but rather as an economic reconfiguration leading to the rise of new regional political formations. See C.A. Bayly, *Rulers, Townsmen and Bazaars : North Indian Society in the Age of British Expansion 1770-1870,* Cambridge, 1983. Muzaffar Alam, 'Eastern India in the Early Eighteenth Century "Crisis" : Some Evidence from Bihar', *Indian Economic and Social History Review,* 28(1), 1991, pp. 43-71. Richard B. Barnett, *North India Between Empires : Awadh, the Mughals, and the British, 1720-1801,* Berkeley, 1980. Sushil Chaudhury, *From Prosperity to Decline : Eighteenth Century Bengal,* Delhi, 1995. Andre Wink, *Land and Sovereignty in India : Agrarian Society and Politics under*

the Eighteenth-Century Maratha Svarajya, Cambridge, 1986. Stewart Gardon, *Marathas, Marauders, and State Formation in Eighteenth-Century India,* OUP, N. Delhi, 1994. Burton Stein, 'State formation and Economy Reconsidered', *Modern Asian Studies,* 19(3), July 1985, pp. 387-413. Frank Perlin, 'Of white Whales and Countrymen in eighteenth Century Maratha Deccan,' *Journal of Peasant Studies*, 5, 1978, pp. 72-237.

3. See S. Bhattacharya, 'Regional Economy 1757-1857 Eastern India', in Dharma Kumar and M. Desai (eds.), *Cambridge Economic History of India,* 1757-1970, Vol. II, Delhi, 1982, pp. 270-95. Om Prakash, 'Trade and Politics in Eighteenth Century Bengal,' in Seema Alavi (ed.), *The Eighteenth Century in India,* Delhi, 1998.
4. C.A. Bayly is main proponent of this idea. See C.A. Bayly, 'Epilogue to the Indian Edition', *Rulers, Townsmen and Bazaars : North Indian Society in the Age of British Expansion 1770-1870,* Indian edn, OUP, Delhi, 1992, pp. 473-99. Rajat Datta, 'Markets, Bullion and Bengal's Commercial Economy : An eighteenth Century Perspective', in Om Prakash and Denys Lombard (eds.), *Commerce and Culture in the Bay of Bengal,* Delhi, 1999, pp. 329-59.
5. See S. Bhattacharya, *The East India Company and the Economy of Bengal, From 1704 to 1740,* London, 1954. Also see *Tapan Raychaudhuri and Irfan Habib*(ed.), *The Cambridge Economic History of India,* Vol. I, Orient Longman, 1984.
6. Francis Buchanan, *An Account of Districts of Bihar and Patna in 1811-12,* Patna.
7. K.K. Datta (ed.), *The Comprehensive History of Bihar*, Vol. III, Part I, Patna, 1976. It is the pioneer work on Bihar based on British primary documents. The book has prepared the ground for the study of political and economic condition during the eighteenth and the nineteenth centuries. Most of the later scholars working on various regions of Bihar have relied heavily upon this work. But the book falls short on some important issues. The authors (of different chapters) have not bothered to discuss anything on the creation of different districts in Bihar. Though the book describes in detail about the political as well as administrative steps taken by the East India Company, but what were the implications of these policies on the geography of the region has not been taken up. Neither is there any discussion on condition of the artisans, their process of manufacturing the products and the organisation of production.
8. H.Q. Naqvi, *Urban Centres and Industries in Upper India* (1556-1803), Calcutta, 1968.
9. R.R. Diwakar, *Bihar Through the Ages,* Calcutta, 1959.
10. Surendra Gopal, *Patna in the Nineteenth Century,* Calcutta, 1982.
11. Qeyamuddin Ahmad (ed.), *Patna Through the Ages : Glimpses of History, Society and Economy,* Patna, 1988.
12. *Ibid*, pp. 179-188. (See a chapter by Ranjan Sinha 'Patna as a Manufacturing and Trading Centre' in the book). So far as the works done exclusively on artisans goes, the title of the two most recent books draw immediate attention. The first of these is by Nita Kumar, *Artisans of Benaras,* OUP, 1986, and the other one is Vijaya Ramaswamy's *Textile and Weavers in Medieval*

South India, Delhi, 1985. The later work does not fit into our area of research since the political and economic order in South India during the seventeenth and the eighteenth centuries was totally different. The book by Nita Kumar, on the other hand, takes up the issue of identity and culture of the artisans living in Benaras and not the economic condition and that too during the twentieth century. She has done more of an empirical study. Such kind of research is not feasible for the period of our research.

13. Amiya Kumar Bagchi's article *'Deindustrialisation in Gangetic Bihar'*, in *Essays in Honour of Prof. S. C. Sarkar*, New Delhi, 1976, p. 502.
14. *Journal of Francis Buchanan Kept during the Survey of the Districts of Patna and Gaya in 1811-12*, edited with notes and introduction by V.H. Jackson, Patna, 1925.
15. *Journal of Francis Buchanan Kept during the Survey of the District of Bhagalpur in* 1810-11, edited with notes and introduction by C.E.A.W. Oldham, Patna 1930, pp. ii-iii, Introduction.
16. R.C. Dutta in *Economic History of India under Early British Rule (1757-1837)*, has used Buchanan's evidence extensively. Also see Amiya Bagchi's article on 'Deindustrialisation in Gangetic Bihar', op. cit.
17. *Fort William -India House Correspondence.* Different volumes of the Indian *Record Series* in edited form are available to us at National Archives of India, N. Delhi.
18. K.K. Datta (ed.), *Catalogue of Patna Commissioner's Records* (1813-1853), Patna, 1963.
19. Ali Mohammad Shah, *Naqsh-e-Paidar*, Patna City, 1924.
20. Syed Badrul Hasan, *Yadgar-e-Rozgar*, Patna City, 1931.

1

THE SYMBIOSIS AND CHANGE IN PHYSICAL ENVIRONMENT

Patna district is of special economic and political significance in the context of a regional history of medieval period. Though Patna as a township is one of the oldest in the world, it went into oblivion after the Mauryas and the Gupta rulers who named it as Patliputra. The city could achieve prominence again only under Sher Shah as a seat of political power during the sixteenth century. In 1541 AD Sher Shah had constructed a fort on the banks of the Ganges in Patna and made it his capital with the name Hazrat Rasulpur. Sher Shah was arguably impressed by the strategic location of Patna, being situated at the confluence of the Ganges and the Gandak. With the establishment of the Mughal rule in Bihar, Patna gained economic prominence as well. In the seventeenth century the European trading companies too preferred this city because of its locational advantage and established their factories here. Despite their colonial rivalry in various parts of the world, one witnesses professional brotherhood and symbiosis among the European trading companies for establishing factories in Patna district. In few years time, the physical environment and the administrative set up of the whole region was completely changed.

Patna district of the Patna Division[1] in Bihar was a part of the province of Bengal[2] during the period of our study. The geographical setting of this region looks more like a rectangle with two sides surrounded by rivers and the other two sides are land locked. It is rounded on the north by the river Ganges, on the south by Gaya district, on the east by Monghyr division and on the west by the river Son which separates it from Shahabad.[3] Its length from east to west is eighty two miles and the breadth varies from twenty eight to forty two miles.[4] It is located between 24°57' and 25°44' North and 84°42 and 86°4' East with an area of 2,075 squares miles.[5] The total length of the Ganges is ninety three miles. The river at Patna is about six hundred yards wide in the cold season, and the stream is then sluggish until it is joined by the Gandak. But from June to September under the combined effect of the melting Himalayan snows and the monsoon rains it becomes a mighty stream several miles wide.[6] The Punpun river enters Patna district near Shehzadpur and it flows in a north easterly direction until it approaches Naubatpur. Here it turns sharply to the east, and joins the Ganges at Fatuha, after flowing for eighty four miles in the district.[7] The river Phalgu enters the district a short distance to the south of Telarha, but soon loses its identity.[8] The Maithun or Mithwain river flows parallel to the Ganges throughout the entire length of the Barh sub-division.[9] The Sakri river enters the district to the south east of Bihar town.[10] The river flows to the north through the south east of the Barh sub-division, from which it enters the Monghyr district.[11] Rajgir hills stands as the southern boundary of the district.[12]

Historical Background

The Mughals, specially Akbar, realised the strategic importance of Bihar and in 1575AD made it a distinct *suba* of his empire.[13] (See Map 1.1) Bihar constituted a strategic area commanding the route to Bengal through the Teliagarhi pass and to Orissa through the uphold of Jharkhand belt. Its boundaries as given in the *Ain-i-Akbari* were nearly the same as present-extending from Rohtas to Teliagarhi pass and from the northern hills to southern hills.[14] Its length from Garhi to Rohtas was 120 kos, its breadth from Tirhut to the northern mountain was 110 kos.[15] The *suba* of Bihar consisted of seven sarkars—Champaran, Saran, Hajipur, Tirhut, Rohtas, Bihar and Monghyr. These were subdivided into 199 parganas yielding a revenue of 22 crore dams or 55 lakh rupees.[16] There were 46 mahals in *suba* of Bihar and the mahals were probably associated with collection of taxes. Patna continued to be its capital and it also became a mint town in 1580 AD, which continued functioning till 1798 AD.

However, the consolidation of the Mughal hold on Bihar was by no means complete. It was confined to few selected and major centres. The imperial authority was frequently challenged in the interiors by the Afghans. The Rebellion of 1580 AD, which was caused by a combination of several administrative, economic and religious factors was spearheaded by these remnants of Pathan power in Bihar.[17] The

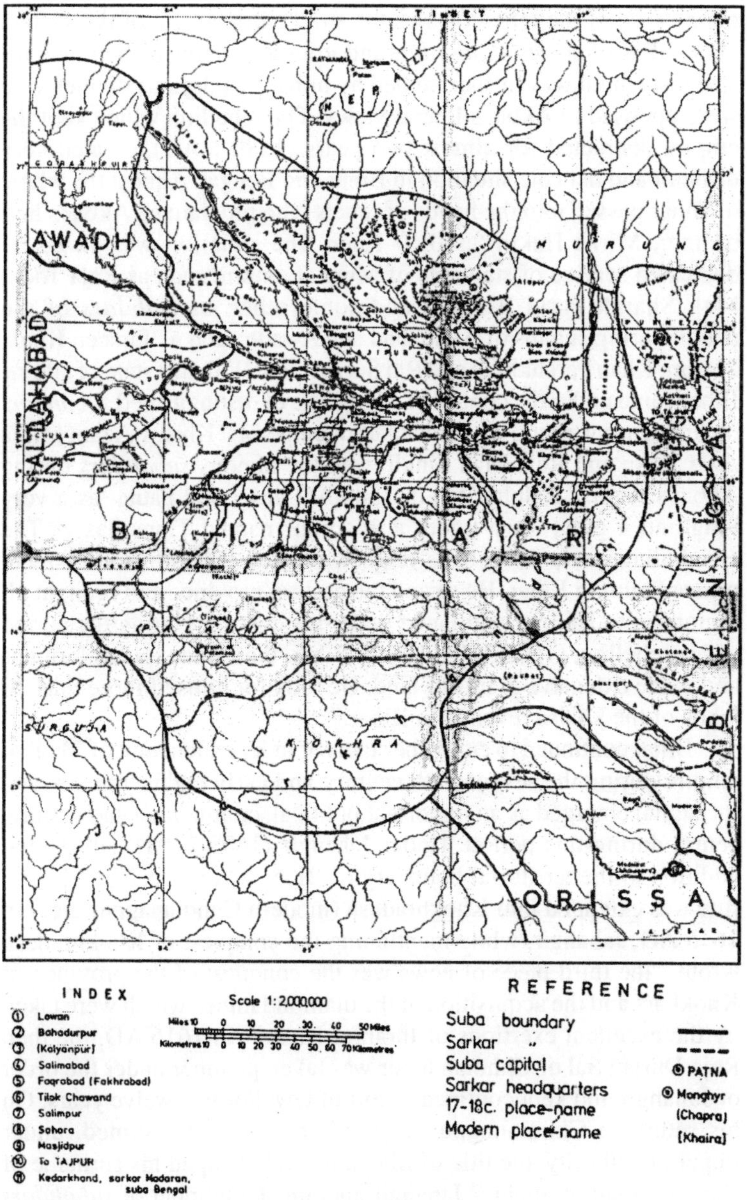

Map 1.1 : Bihar *Suba* under Akbar

Based on Irfan Habib's *An Atlas of the Mughal Empror,* OUP, 1982, Sheet No. 10

main cause of the rebellion was the strict enforcement of the system of branding of horses of *jagirdars* and strict accounting of their income. The discontent was further fanned by unhappy religious divines who were opposed to Akbar's liberal views. The rebellion which kept the empire distracted for almost two years (1580-1 AD), created very difficult and delicate situation in Bihar and Bengal. Almost the whole of Bihar passed into the hands of rebels who proclaimed Akbar's half brother, Mirza Hakim as their ruler. The situation was saved by dedicated service of stalwarts of Mughal empire such as Raja Todar Mal, Shaikh Farid Bukhari and some other *mansabdars* of the neighbouring subahs of Allahabad and Awadh such as Tarseen Khan, Masum Khan Farankhudi and Rai Surjan etc.[18] With this state of affairs, Bihar came under the control of a long line of distinguished *subahdars* including princes and close relatives of emperors. Khan-i-Azam Mirza Aziz Koka and Raja Man Singh were the famous *subahdars* during Akbar's reign.[19] Ralph Fitch in 1583 AD described Patna 'as a very long and a great town under a governor named Tipperdas'.[20] The concluding years of Akbar's reign witnessed the intrusion of rebel prince Salim in Bihar. He seized the eastern province and brought all regions upto Hajipur and Patna under his control. During the period of his rebellion (1600-1604 AD) in Bihar, the Prince issued farmans and made extensive grants of land. He took for himself more than 30 lakhs of the khalsa revenue in Bihar.[21]

Bihar continued to enjoy the status of independent unit of Mughal empire during the seventeenth century and early eighteenth century. Its capital emerged as an important political, commercial and cultural centre during this period. Under Jahangir (1605-27AD) substantial addition to the territorial boundary of Bihar was made. The Mughal rule was extended into Khokhradesh (modern Chhotanagpur area) in 1615 AD. Jahangir, while mentioning the conquest of Khokhradesh wrote, "the third piece of news was the conquest of the province of Khokhars and the acquisition of the diamond mines which were taken by the excellent exertions of Ibrahim Khan.[22] In 1616 AD, the then Raja Durjan Sal of Chhotanagpur was taken prisoner under the order of Jahangir and kept confined in fort of Gwalior for twelve years. On his return to Chhotanagpur, after his release, he assumed, under imperial authority, the title of Maharaja and changed his surname of Rai into Shah or Shahi.[23] Jahangir appointed a number of *subahdars* for efficient administration of Bihar. The province remained under Afzal Khan, the son of Abul Fazal till 1612 AD. In 1612 AD, Patna was sacked by the pretender Khusru who had himself proclaimed emperor in governor's place.[24] When Robert Hughes and Parker came to Patna 1612 AD, the *subahdar* of Bihar was Muqarrab Khan. He was on good terms with the English merchants in Bihar. His association with them dated back to the period of his governorship at Surat. Robert Hughes, in one of his letters has referred Muqarrab Khan as one of the best patrons of the English. He left Patna in 1621AD, when prince Parwez, the second of the five sons of Jahangir obtained Bihar as *Jagir*.[25] Prince Parwez was first Mughal prince of royal blood who came to rule Bihar. Several other followed him which led Captain Hamilton to describe 'Patna as the residence of the Prince of Bengal who is always of royal blood'.[26] Prince Parwez stayed in Bihar till April, 1623 AD. Bihar for some time was also occupied by rebellious Prince Khurram who with the help of Raja Bhim seized Patna without any opposition. Prince Khurram after unsuccessful rebellion in the Deccan had come to the eastern province. However, the victory was short lived and a crushing defeat was inflicted on him by Prince Parwez on the bank of river Tons near Bahadurpur on 26th Oct 1624 AD. Those soldiers who had deserted Prince Khurram in battle came to Patna ahead of the prince and put the city to fire, pillage and plunder.[27]

The general prosperity of Shah Jahan's reign, filtered in Bihar too, particularly under the *subahdar* Saif Khan (1628-30 AD). He proved to be one of the ablest governors in Bihar under the Mughals. During the four years of his governorship, Bihar had witnessed an era of peace, prosperity and splendour. Peter Mundy who came to Patna in 1632 AD, shortly after Saif's transfer to Allahabad, makes mention of the esteem to which Saif was held by people of Bihar and contrasts the 'tyrannical and the exacting regime' of his successor Abdullah Khan Firuz Jung.[28] Peter Mundy's account has given valuable information which has helped in reconstructing the history of Bihar. The closing years of the reign of Shah Jahan, witnessed the painful drama of a war among his sons. There is plenty of source material relating to the history of the struggle for succession to the throne, but the references relating to the affairs of Bihar during the period are at times confusing and even misleading.[29] Alivardi Khan was the governor of Bihar during the last years of Shah Jahan's rule.

Under Aurangzed, Bihar continued to remain a separate province. The final round of Mughal expansion in eastern India took place in

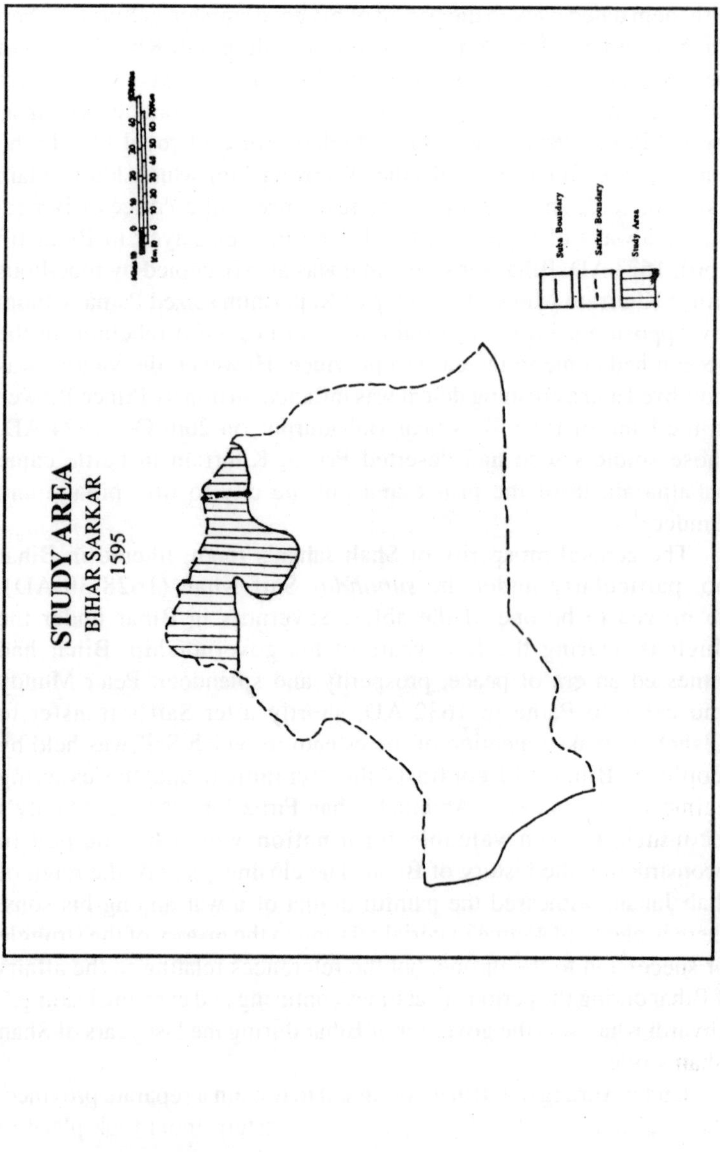

Map 1.2 : Bihar under the Mughals

Aurangzeb's reign (1658-1707 AD) and it found its echo in Bihar too, when Daud Khan Quraishi, the *subahdar* (1659-64AD) attacked Palamau fort and occupied the area.[30] Daud Khan was succeeded by Lashkar Khan and it was during his rule that the European travellers Tavernier and Bernier came to Patna. They give us valuable information about the administrative division, revenue of the province, its capital, its governors and some of the manner and customs. 'Patna or Beara' says Bernier who alone gives the name of 'Lashkar Khan' as governor of Patna 'has 8 *sarkars* and 245 *parganas* yielding 95 lacs 80,000 rupees'.[31] Patna experienced devastating famine during the governorship of Ibrahim Khan (1668-73 AD.) John Marshall, the Dutch Traveller De Graffic and Thomas Bowrey have given graphic descriptions of the horrible scenes they witnessed and heard of during the famine.[32] Shortly before Aurangzeb's death, Bihar was given in January 1703 AD to Prince Azim-us Shan as an appanage to the governorship of Bengal which he had held since 1996 AD. Patna during his three years stay took a new shape and a new name Azimabad. Aurangzeb who had retained the control over affairs of state to the very end, could not evade fatricidal struggle. His sons' and gradsons' ambition to gain the throne became apparent. Niccola Manucci observed : "The great age of the emperor who is more than 86 years old and the ambition to gain the throne continuously displayed by his sons and grandson give rise to the apprehension of some catastrophe quite as tragic that supervening at the close of Shah Jahan's reign"[33] The Emperor Aurangzeb after having spent a great part of his life in administering the Mughal empire was over taken by the fate. Meanwhile, the news of the emperor's illness having spread all over the empire every one made haste to secure himself in his post by every means in his power.[34] Muazzam who had acquired considerable power in north India came out successful in this struggle and ascended the throne under the title of Bahadur Shah (1707-12AD).

By the beginning of eighteenth century Bihar figured prominently in the general political history of the country.[35] The people and the resources of Bihar played a decisive role in it. Farukhsiyar's (1712-19AD) bid for the imperial throne was made from Patna and he succeeded largely due to help of *subahadar* of Bihar Hussain Ali Khan. The swift catastrophic political changes not only generated the forces of lawlessness and disorder but also hastened the disintegration of the empire. Bihar was no exception to the refractioriness and lawlessness prevailing all over the country.[36] The increasing commercial activity of the English East India Company and its greater involvement in the political affairs of the country had also its share in it. Patna came to serve as a sounding board for information regarding the court politics at Delhi.[37] All the news regarding the political development at Delhi reached Hugli councillors of English East India Company through Patna. The hold of the central government over the *suba* Bihar slowly eroded. The last of separate governors of Bihar was Fakhr-ud-daula, whom the emperor dismissed and from that time Bihar came under the control of the governors of Bengal.[38] In 1734 AD Alivardi Khan became the governor of Bihar. Yusuf Ali Khan writes, in consideration of the fact that difficulties and the problems of the province (of Bihar) could be solved by only one man (that is Alivardi) who was the embodiment of so many virtues Shuja-ul-Dawalah ordered him (Alivardi) to go to Bihar (as his deputy).[39] The inevitable results of these conditions were the battle of Plassey (1757 AD), the battle of Buxar (1764 AD) and the grant of *diwani* to the Company (1765 AD). In the middle of the eighteenth century the province of Bihar passed through troubled times. After Robert Clive's victory at Plassey, for several years Patna became the centre of operation of British troops. In 1763 AD, Patna came under Mir Kasim but its fate was sealed after the battle of Buxar. From that time Bihar, with the rest of Bengal, came under the suzerainty of the English East India Company.[40]

For the survey of Patna as a district, we have to depend mainly on Mughal accounts, since survey operation could commence under the British rule only in the year 1835.[41] In fact, in Bihar the survey work was done mainly during 1840s and 1850s.[42] The maps prepared before 1850 were rough and mere eye-sketches which did not show the boundary between the estates.[43] A comparison of the names of the *pargana* as given in these maps and in *Ain-i-Akbari*[44] shows that while some *parganas* included in this district during the nineteenth century were not to be found during *Ain's* times, while a few *parganas* listed in the *Ain's* are not found in the first. But this difference is evident only because of the change in the names of the *parganas* over the years. In reality, the *parganas* created during Mughal period even continued during the eighteenth and nineteenth century with new names for a few and a majority of the names remaining unchanged (Table 1.1).[45]

Table 1.1 : *Parganas* Constituting Patna District in 1811-12

Parganas in Buchanan's times (C. 1811-12)	*Parganas in Ain's (C.1595)*	*Remarks (Changes, if any)*
1. Haveli-Behar	Bihar bahaveli	None
2. Biswak	Biswak or Basok	None
3. Ballia	Baha or ballia	None
4. Baikunthpur	Not mentioned	Created during seventeenth-eighteenth century[46]
5. Bhimpur	Bhimpur	None
6. Gayaspur	Ghiaspur	None
7. Maner	Muner	None
8. Masaurha	Masodha	None
9. Azimabad[47]	Patna	Change in name[48]
10. Phulwari	Phulwari	None
11. Pilich	Palach	None
12. Rajgriha	Rajgir	None
13. Sanda	Sandah	None
14. Telarah	Tiladah	None
15. Shahjahanpur	Not mentioned	Created in modern times[49]
16. Dinapur	Not mentioned	Created in mid eighteenth century as a Cantonment of the British East India Company's army[50]

Out of the above mentioned sixteen *parganas* during Buchanan's survey, thirteen were present during Akbar's reign.[51] Only three new *parganas* i.e. Baikunthpur, Shahjahanpur, and Dinapur seem to have been formed in the later period. Of these three, we have not come across any evidence regarding Baikunthpur and Shahjahanpur as to why these new *parganas* were formed. But for Dinapur we do have the evidence to suggest that it was created as a new settlement for the British army.[52] Since the majority of the *parganas* remained unchanged from Mughal period to British period some degree of administrative continuity is reflected.[53] A detailed analysis of the administrative history will tell us about the change in the administrative structure with the change in the administrative authority. We would also see as to how and why Patna district as such was created?

Administrative History of the Region

With the decline of the Mughal power in the early eighteenth century Patna had slipped into the hands of the Nawab of Bengal. The Nawabs maintained the commercial prosperity of Patna, even though it suffered extensively in the first half of the century on account of feuds in the Nawab's family and the Maratha raiders.[54] But after the battle of Plassey in 1757, the English East India Company became powerful and tried to monopolise the ongoing trade in and around Patna. This led to a conflict with the Nawab of Bengal, Mir Qasim, who had come forward to protect the interest of the local merchants. Mir Qasim also got the support of the Mughal emperor, Shah Alam II and the nawab of Oudh, Shujauddaulah, in his bold effort to challenge the British. However, the English again won the battle that followed and became the de-facto and after some time de -jure ruler of Bihar, Bengal and Orissa.[55] Now the English were politically supreme and were able to oust all other European business competitors and the local Indian merchants. How they were successful in partially monopolising[56] the trading and related activities, we shall discuss it in the third section of the chapter. What is important here to note is that the whole political and economic conditions had changed and this affected the character of Patna both as a city and as a district.

The physical shape of Patna changed according to the requirements of the British, though the old *parganas* were retained, as we have seen in the earlier section. The British did so because they "....did not want to live in the old town. They desired to maintain their distance from the local population. They dislike living in the old city which was congested and unclean and the chances of clashes with the local population were greater. They did not like to develop a city in the Dinapore Cantt or in its close provincity. Hence, they decided to develop the area midway between the Western ramparts of the old town and Dinapore along the river bank".[57] A letter dated 29th January, 1766, from Fort William to India House makes the objective of the East India Company all the more clear. Para 44 and 45 of the letter says, "Taking into consideration the expediency of erecting cantonments and establishing headquarters at Patna for the greater security of the provinces and facility of sending off detachments to assist in the collections, or suppress such tumults as may arise in different parts of the country, we referred the same to the judgement of the field officers".[58] For such a convenience of administration the company was even ready to spend as many as three lacs of rupee.[59] The letter further says, "The very incommodious situation of the Chief arid Council at Patna since the demolition of the factory by Cossim Aly (Mir Qasim), determined us to convert the kella (fort) into a factory house for the greater security of your investment, as well as convenience of your servants, ...but here we think it necessary to remark that we never proposed to incur the expense of building regular fortifications, but only to render the place defensible against slight and sudden attacks".[60]

In the meanwhile, towards the end of 1769 signs of impending famine began to appear in Bihar,[61] and the need for a change in the system of administration was felt. In the same year English supervisors were appointed all through the *diwani* portion of the land. But the arrangement proved abortive.[62] In September; 1770 two provincial councils (Controlling Councils of Revenue) were formed to supervise revenue matters, one at Murshidabad for Bengal and the other at Patna for Bihar.[63] This laid the foundation for the formation of modern Patna district. Hitherto the administrations of civil and criminal justice had been included in the Revenue Council at Patna. In 1790 the revenue department commenced recording its judicial business separately. This arrangement continued till the end of April 1793, when as a result of the reform introduced from 1st May, 1793, all proceedings regarding the administration of civil and criminal justice began to be recorded in a separate judicial series, and thus a separate judicial department came into existence[64] Thus, in 1793, Patna became a separate judicial district also. In 1798, the narrow strip of land between Maner and Phatuha along the bank of the Ganges was separated from district of Bihar and placed under the Magistrate of the city of Patna.[65] In 1825, the Magistrate reported that the prevalence of thugi in barah rendered the place inaccessible from Gaya for the greater part of the year and so a new Patna district, with concurrent civil and revenue jurisdiction was carved out of the northern portion of Bihar district in the same year.[66] FrancisBuchanan, who was appointed by the East India Company to make a survey of the districts of Bihar and Patna in 1811-12, wrote : "The survey, which I have now made, includes the districts under the authority of two judges and magistrates; one who preside over the city of Patna and a small adjacent territory, and the other who presides over what remains after several dismemberments of the district of Bihar".[67]

A description of the circumstances under which the East India

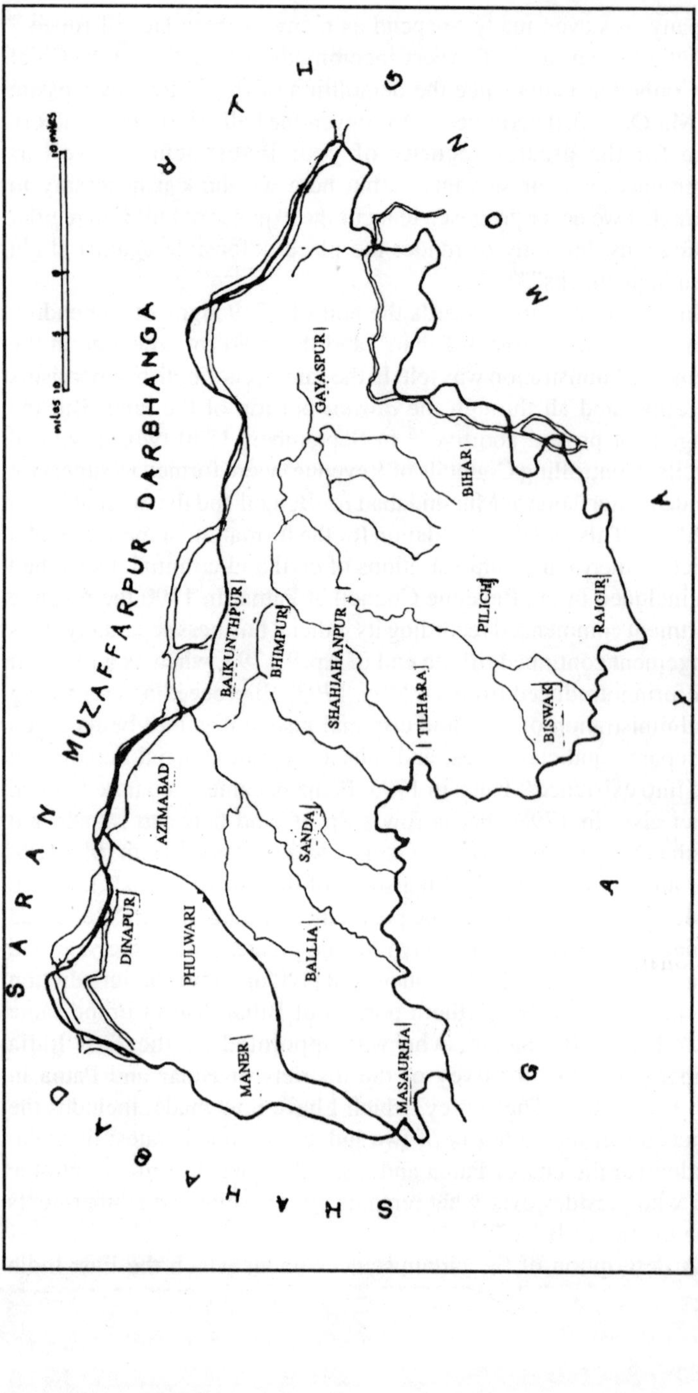

Map 1.3 : Patna District (1811-12)

Company was able to manipulate the things in its favour and acquired the exclusive rights of revenue administration in its favour will be worth examining. As with the acquisition of diwani, the " ....Control of the Council of Revenue, the Provincial Councils, the appointment of European supervisors in the district and their substitution by Indian naibs[68] became imminent. On the one hand, the company was gradually getting the administrative rights from the Mughal emperor and its allies, after the battle of Buxar in 1764, but at the same time it continued with its criticism of the Indian rulers for their misgovernment in Bengal and Bihar.[69]

To regulate the administrative affairs in Bengal and Bihar and to safeguard the interest of the Company, the Court of Directors appointed Lord Clive as Governor of Bengal and President of Select Committee in Calcutta with Verilst, Sykes, Summer and General Carnac as its members.[70] On 12th August 1765, Clive was able to acquire the diwani of Bihar and Orissa[71] from the Mughal emperor, Shah Alam II. It is interesting to note that such a settlement in Bengal was in contemplation as early as 1758 during Clive's early stay as Governor. At that time the imperial Court in Delhi was extremely desirous of appointing the President of the Calcutta council as 'the kings's Dan' (Diwan), but the President and council were afraid to cause the Nawab " ....any dissatisfaction at a time when our small force is engaged another way".[72] In January 1759, Clive wrote to Pitt mentioning the same objection "...so large a sovereignty may possibly be an object too extensive for a mercantile company; and it is to be feared that they are not of themselves able, without the nation's assistance to maintain so wide a dominion"[73] He asked whether the execution of a design that may hereafter be still carried to greater lengths, be worthy of the government's taking it into hand. Pitt's reply stressed that such revenue would endanger our liberties. Clive in reaction to the offer of diwani from the imperial court clearly indicates a definite trend towards the acquisition of political power by the East India Company.[74] The company was not satisfied with the defect ascendancy which it had secured in the administration of Bengal and the increasing commercial privileges enjoyed by it and its servants.[75] Even Under Vansittart (1760-64) the option of the acquisition of diwani was not preferred. Vansittart was anxious to avoid any measure which was likely to be taken amiss by Mir Qasim or other Nawabs.[76] It was only under Clive, when he became the Governor of Bengal for the second time[72] that a policy of weakening the nawab was followed. He thought that[77] ....the

Nawab could be reduced to a political phantom only when the company had direct control over the collection of revenue[78] and this meant the acquisition of diwani.

The diwani grant secured immense advantages to the English, mainly in terms of revenue. However, the company always tried to give an impression that they have acquired the diwani just to control the prevailing anarchic situation. Referring to various abuses prevailing in Bengal Clive wrote to the Court of Directors on 30th September, 1765 a detailed note which also explains his designs as how to govern these provinces. In view of the intrinsic value of this note it is appended in full at the end of this paper(See Appendix 1).

The company's administration attached great importance to the collection of the land revenue, and its earliest measures were naturally directed towards obtaining a correct idea of the total amount of the land revenue and the methods and machinery employed for collecting it in full on proper time. One essential work in this connection was the collection of accurate information about the areas and boundaries of the villages and mahals within them. In the official correspondence relating to the survey operations for this purpose, it is stated that the purpose of these surveys in the permanently settled districts of Bengal and Bihar was to determine the relation between land and *jama* by ascertaining the area and boundaries of the mahals.[79]

It is difficult to work out a definite physical boundary of Patna district during the period of our study. What we can do, therefore, is to restrict ourselves to the study of the boundary specified by Buchanan in his survey report. In fact, Buchanan seems to be very uncomfortable while showing the jurisdiction of the Magistrate of Patna. "There is a good deal of difficulty in ascertaining the boundaries of Patna. To exclude what is without the walls would reduce its dimensions to a trifle, while the suburbs are built in a very straggling ill defined manner. I find it most suitable for my purpose to include the whole of that part of Patna pargana, or Haveli Azimabad, that is under the jurisdiction of a Kotwal and 15 Darogahs, who are appointed to superintendent police of the sixteen wards (muhallah), into which the above mentioned extent is divided".[80] Buchanan defines the jurisdiction of the Magistrate of Patna to the city of Patna,[81] Phatuha,[82] Naubatpur division,[83] Bankipore Jaywar division,[84] and Sherpur division.[85] According to him the extent of Patna along the Ganges extended upto20 square miles,[86] and if the suburbs and Jafar Khan's garden were included, it had a length of nine miles[87] along the river bank. Marufganj, which was a great suburb and the principal market containing many storied houses of grain, was situated on the eastern end of the city.[88] Buchanan says that the eastern part of the town was raised "...in consequence of the European settlement and the houses of the Europeans were scattered throughout, chiefly along the bank of the river.....Notwithstanding that this is one of the chief European settlements in India, being the seat of a court of appeals, of a city Judge and Magistrate, of the Collector of a fertile district, of a custom house, of a commercial resident, of an opium agent, and of provincial battalion, the number of European houses is trifling, and they are so scattered that they make no show"[84]

The Dyarchy in Patna District

In August 1765, Clive obtained from the Mughal emperor at Allahabad the formal grant of the diwani of Bengal, Bihar and Orissa. After this, he made important changes in civil administration. In 1766, a council of three was appointed consisting of Mr. Middleton, Chief of the Factory, Dheraj Narain, the Maharaja Sitab Rai. In September 1766, Thomas Rumbold was appointed Chief of Patna in Mr. Middleton's place, and Dheraj Narain was removed. Sitab Rai was now the Company's Naib diwan for Bihar, and his place as agent of the emperor was taken by the Nawab Reza Quli Khan (Manir-ud-daula). Fumbold carried on the administration jointly with Sitab Rai until he went to England in 1769, and after that he was succeeded by James Alexander.

Towards the end of 1769 signs of impending famine began to appear in surrounding regions of Patna district. In January 1770 famine had proceeded so far that Sitab Rai reported that fifty persons were dying daily of starvation in Patna.[90] Consequently, a change was made in the system of administration by the appointment of the Revenue Council of Patna which consisted of James Alexander as President, with Robert Palok and George Vansittart as members, with authority over the Naib diwan in revenue matters. However, Sitab Rai remained in general charge of the nizamat administration. Thus, the Council at once began to interfere actively in revenue affairs and even went to the extent of fixing the maximum rent at nine sixteenth of the produce.

In 1772, the directors issued an order for the removal of Sitab Rai. He was publicly removed from his office and sent to Calcutta for an enquiry into his administration.[91] He emerged from the enquiry with honour and in the end was reinstated, but he died shortly after his return to Patna in 1773. Thereupon, his son Kallian Singh was appointed Rai-raiyan of Bihar, with an annual salary of fifty thousand rupees, and the Naibs of Sitab Rai were reappointed. The general revenue administration remained in the hands of the Council, of which successive Presidents were Richard Barwell (1771), John Graham (1772), George Vansittart (1772), George Hurst 1773), Thomas lane (1773), Robert Palk (1775), Isaac Sage (1776), Ewan Law (1777) and William Maxwell (1780).

The administration of the revenue under Council was unsatisfactory and so change in the system was made in 1781.[92] The Council was abolished and the farm of the whole of Bihar province was taken by Rai-raiyan. William Maxwell who died in August 1781, and after an interval of two months, during which James Lindsay Ross acted as Revenue Chief, was succeeded by William Augustus Brooke. In 1783, John Shore came to Patna and made a re-settlement of land revenue for a term of three years. Shore merely made a farming settlement based on rough knowledge of assets.

In July 1787, the office of Revenue Chief was abolished and Thomas Law became Collector of the district. He conceived the scheme of making a permanent settlement with the local zamindars and promptly carried it into effect.[93] The Decennial Settlement (for ten years) of the whole district was completed by 1790. *Parganas* settled wholly or chiefly with zamindars were Baikunthpur (Udwant Singh), Masaurha (Jaswant Singh), Shahjahanpur and Tilhara (Mir Muhammad Baker Khan). Rajgir remained with Muhammad Yahya and part of Biswak and Bhimpur with Manir-ud-duaula's family. Sanda and Balia were held earlier by farmers with a permanent lease, but when the farmers defaulted these *parganas* were settled with maliks.[94] The decennial settlement was made permanent in 1793.

Thus, by the end of the eighteenth century, gradually the power of the local revenue officers was seized and the British administration was successful in determining the amount and way of collection of revenue by the settlement with local zaminadars.

The Symbiosis

Though Buchanan seems to be reluctant to the fact that Europeans had settled in Patna district in large number, there is no doubt that various European companies had established their factories and trading houses here. Of these, the Dutch, the French and the English are important, who began their operations in Patna in the seventeenth century. Patna was then one of the most important and biggest commercial centres in eastern India which had attracted the attention of European merchants owing particularly to its cotton productions, saltpetre and opium. The discovery of gun-powder and the growing use of it in warfare greatly accelerated the demand of Bihar saltpetre due to its superior quality and cheapness.[90] During the seventeenth and eighteenth centuries, the activities of the European companies were guided by constant rivalry, in which the East India Company emerged successful at the end.

It is not known exactly as to when the first Dutch factory in Patna came into existence. However, it is believed that " ....a factory had been set up at Patna in 1638 but closed the same year for reasons of economy",[96] sometime between 1645 and 1651, the Patna factory was reestablished.[97] Under Mughal emperor Farrukhsiyar, the Dutch were given the right to use the mint and the privilege of occupying the house of Nurullah Khan at Patna free of charge as residence or a store house, provided it was not fortified or equipped with artillery.[98] With the decline of Dutch power in Europe, the Dutch East India Company began to fall rapidly even in Bengal. S. Bhatacharya believes that two comparative position of the English East India Company and the Dutch East India Company in the early eighteenth century undoubtedly establish the superior position of the English.[99]

The Dutch, however, had monopolised the production in the seventeenth century and gave the English a tough time in establishing themselves at Patna. Apart from the commercial rivalry an important "...cause of friction between the companies was the uncommon scarcity of weavers"[100] which in fact adversely affected the foreign trade of all the European companies. The Dutch complained that the weavers engaged by them were enticed away by the agents of the English company and the weavers supplied clothes to none except the English.[101]

This reflects the bargaining potential of the weavers as artisans. The Dutch or the English were not in a position to produce the clothes on their own during the seventeenth to eighteenth centuries. The weavers of Patna realised it very well that the Europeans were at the receiving end and so exploited the situation to their own advantage. The rivalry among the different European Companies may well have been another supporting factor in this regard. But it is here when the Indians failed to foresee the future. Once the monopoly of any single company is established after a phase of cut-throat competition, which the English East India Company successfully did, that company would wreck the back of these weavers.

Despite their rivalry, the Dutch and the English East India Companies acted in co-operation when it came to be the matter of common interest in India. The Dutch generally joined with the English in trying to keep out other European rivals. In 1795, owing to French-Dutch war, the Dutch possessions in India were placed under the protection of the English government for their safety against the French. On 14th August, 1795, the Magistrate of Patna, Henry Dauglas, was directed to take over the Dutch factory at Patna.[102] The Dutch factory at Patna was restored to them in 1817. However, "in 1824-25, the Dutch possessions in India were finally ceded to the English government"[103]

In comparison to the Dutch, the French were more formidable rivals of the English. Commercial jealousy was the basic factor in their hostility which is fully borne out by the directions of the directors "that you live on good terms with the French so far as may be practicable, but is no less our wish to supplant them, as far as we may safely and prudently do it, in their commerce.[104] The East India Company took all precautionary measures to counteract the French, although these precautions proved to be unnecessary as the French had no effective means at the time to disturb the peace of their English rivals in India, particularly in view of the lack of any support from Indian powers.[105] It was in 1674 that Shaista Khan, then governor of Bengal, had permitted the French to establish settlements.[106] In 1693, the French succeeded in obtaining a *farman* from the emperor Auangzeb with permission to trade in Bengal, Bihar and Orissa on the same pattern as the Dutch,[107] During the first half of the eighteenth century, the French factory at Patna had become an important centre of trade.[108] But by the end of the century, the French establishment here was captured by the English, influenced by the revolutionary and Napoleonic wars in Europe. The Commanding Officer at Dinapur detached a force to take possession of the French factory at Patna and other French dependencies of Bihar.[109]

Like the Dutch, the French too joined hands with the English when their interest clashed with the government on the purchase of saltpetre. The English, the Dutch and the French entered into a tripartite agreement to frustrate the designs of the government.[110] Again in 1738, when Patna was threatened by an inroad of the Marathas, Duplex proposed that the chiefs of the three European companies at Patna should unite and act jointly in case of an invasion.[111]

As far as the history of English factory in Patna goes it could be traced to the early seventeenth century. The exact date of the establishment of a permanent factory at Patna is not known. In 1632, an attempt was made by the English to establish a factory here, when the prospects of trade in Gujarat were seriously affected by the devastating Gujarat famine of 1630-3131.[112]

In 1651, the English East India Company set up a factory at Hugli and a trading agency at Patna and in 1657, they were able to establish a permanent factory in Patna.[113] However, the English always had to face the blunt of the Indian rulers and Nawabs and their factories were closed time and again, for example, once in 1702 as a result of the execution of Aurangzeb's *farman* of 1701 interdicting European trade in India, the Patna factory was closed. Again during the political convulsions of 1756-57 the Patna factory of the English was closed. It was, however, re-established in August 1757.[114]

By the end of the eighteenth century, the English East India Company had managed to get a monopolistic control over all the factory production in Patna district. The company's wishes were fulfilled byway of three factors. One, the political situation in Europe was favourable to the English. Secondly, the English were successful in creating a joint front with the French and the Dutch cornering the commercial rivalry among themselves. There is no denying the fact that in relation to country powers the Europeans were occasionally guided by some sort of symbiosis and professional brotherhood. The third contributing factor was the grant of diwani to the East India Company and the gradual increase in political power of the company.

NOTES

1. *Imperial Gazetteers,* Vol. XX, 1908, p. 54.
2. *Provincial Gazetteers of India, Bengal,* Vol. II, p. 3.
3. O' Malley, *Bihar and Orissa District Gazetteers*, Patna, 1924, p. 1 . These adjoining areas of Shahabad west of the river Son are now called district Arrah and Sasaram.
4. Ibid., p. 1.
5. *Imperial Gazetteers,* p. 54
6. O' Malley, *op.cit.,* p. 4.
7. *Ibid.*, p. 6
8. *Ibid.*, p. 7
9. *Ibid.*, p. 7
10. *Ibid.*, p. 8
11. *Ibid.*, p. 8

12. *Ibid.*, p. 8
13. Abul Fazal, *Ain-i-Akbari*, p. 129; Rajiv Nain Prasad, 'Glimpses into the history of Medieval Bihar', in P.N. Ojha (ed.), *Bihar Past and Present,* p. 47.
14. Q. Ahmad, *Patna Through the Ages,* Patna, 1988, p. 70.
15. Abul Fazal, *op. cit.,* p. 162.
16. Bhagwant Sahai and Sachidanand Sahai, (eds.) *Bihar Past and Present,* p. 65.
17. B.P. Ambasthya, 'Restoration and early phase of Mughal rule in Bihar (1574-1614 AD)', S.H. Askari and Q Ahmed, (ed.) *The Comprehensive History of Bihar,* p. 117
18. Bhagwant Sahai and Sachidanand Sahai, *op. cit.,* p. 65.
19. *Ibid.*
20. 'Tipper Das' was probably Rai Patar Das the joint Dewan of Muzzafar Khan, the governor of Bengal and Bihar, as cited in NN Raye, *op. cit.*, p. 43.
21. P.N. Ojha, *Bihar Past and Present*, p. 48.
22. Jahangir, *Tuzuk-i-Jahangiri,* (tr.) Alexander Rogers and (ed.) Henry Beveridge, Book I, pp. 314-15.
23. S.C. Roy, *The Oraons of Chotanagpur,* p. 42.
24. J. Houlton, *Bihar, The Heart of India*, pp. 16-17.
25. N.N. Raye, *The Annals of the English Settlement in Bihar*, p. 48.
26. Hamilton, *A new Account of East Indies,* Chap. XXIV as cited in N.N. Raye *op.cit.*
27. S.H. Askari and Q. Ahmad, *op. cit.,* p. 145.
28. R.R. Diwakar, *Bihar Through the Ages*, p. 494.
29. S.H. Askari and Q. Ahmed, (ed.) *The Comprehensive History of Bihar, Vol. II, Part II,* Patna, 1976, p. 152.
30. Bhagwant Sahai and Sachdidanand Sahai, *op. cit.,* p. 65.
31. Travels of Bernier, cited in Syed Hasan Askari's, *Medieval Bihar (Sultanate and Mughal Period,* p. 154.
32. R.R. Diwakar, *op. cit.,* pp. 497-8.
33. Niccolao Manucci, *Storia do Mogor or Mughal India (1953-1708 AD),* vol. III, (Eng. tr.) William Irvine, p. 173.
34. Seid Gholam Hossien Khan, *The Seir Mutaqherin,* vol. I, (tr.) Nota-Manus, p. 4.
35. Bhagwant Sahai and Sachidanand Sahai, *op.cit.*, p. 67.
36. R.R. Diwakar, *op. cit.,* p. 504.
37. Q. Ahmad, *Patna through the Ages,* p. 76.
38. John Houlton, *op.cit.,* pp. 16-17.
39. Yusuf Ali Khan *Tarikh-i-Bangala-i-Mahabat Jangi.,* Abdus Subhan, (tr.), p. 5.
40. John Houlton, *op. cit.,* p. 18.
41. Askari and Ahmad (ed.), *op. cit,* Appendix IV, p. 590.
42. I*bid.,* p. 590.
43. See *Catalogue of the Historical Maps of the Survey of India (1700-1900),* National Archives of India, N. Delhi. In none of the maps covering the period of our study do we find any clear-cut boundary of Patna district.
44. See Irfan Habib's *An Atlas of the Mughal Empire,* Sheet 10A, Oxford University Press, Delhi, 1986; and B.P. Ambasthya (ed.), *Beans'*

Contributions to the Political Geography of the Subah of Awadh, Bihar, Bengal and Orissa in the Age of Akbar, Patna, 1976, pp. 23-24. Also see *Ain-i Akbari,* tr. by H.S. Jarrett, pp. 165-166.

45. Since we are concentrating our study on the modern division of Patna district for an indepth understanding of change and continuity in these regions we have tried to figure out a comparison with the mahals or parganas as mentioned in the *Ain-i-Akbari*. See Jharrett's translation of *Ain-i-Akbari*, Delhi 1978, p. 166, for the list of parganas as existing in 1811-12 see Francis Buchanan, *An Account of the Districts of Bihar and Patna in 1811-1812,* pp. 571-609
46. Irfan Habib, op. cit.
47. "Among the *parganas* of Bihar, the pargana of Azimabad (old name of Patna during the eighteenth century), situated on the north-western portion of the district on the bank of the Ganges, was surveyed by Lieut. W. Maxwell, Revenue Surveyor, during 1841-42. The map drawn by him of the *paragana* which included the capital town Patna, shows the cluster of buildings spread along the southern bank of the Ganges. This is in sharp contrast to rural areas covering the southern portions. Some of the important localities shown are Fatuha Khas, Shamspur Fatuha, Fatehpur Kelam, Mirchi, Mohiuddinpur Khera, Chowk, Saleh, Sohangi Azim Chowk, Qazi Qeyamuddin Chowk, Simli Muradpur, Makhadumpur, Salehpur, Punadeh, Jethuli Khurd etc. In the town area, Sandalpur Kalam, Dhawalpura, Aimma Ranno Bibi could be seen. cf. *CHB* Vol. II, part II, Appendix IV pp. 591-92 Also see map of *pargana* Azimbad and index map to Patna district.
48. In the early eighteenth century (C. 1704) it was named Azimabad during the governorship of Azimuddin Azim-us-shan, the grand-son of Aurangzeb. See O' malley, *op. cit.,* p. 23.
49. Irfan Habib, *op. cit.,* Sheet 10A and Notes.
50. *Provincial Gazetteers of India, Bengal,* Vol. II, p. 19.
51. Although Askari & Ahmad in the Appendix to their *CHB*, Vol. II, Part II, p. 593, mention that "the then district of Patna which included parts of the present Gaya and Monghyr districts had 12 parganas in it".
52. *Provincial Gazetteers of India Bengal,* Vol. II, p. 19.
53. *CHB*, Vol. II, Part II, p. 591.
54. Surendra Gopal, *Patna in the nineteenth century : A socio-economic profile,* Calcutta, 1982, p. 2.
55. K.K. Datta (ed.), *CHB*, Vol. III, Part I, Patna, 1976, p. 116.
56. Debendra Bijoy Mitra, *The Cotton Weavers of Bengal (1757-1833)*, Calcutta, 1978, p. 5.
57. cf. Surendra Gopal, *op-cit,* p. 3.
58. C.S. Srinivasachari (ed.), *India Record Series : Fort William-India House Correspondence*, Vol. IV (1764-66), Delhi 1962, p. 372.
59. *Ibid*, p. 372.
60. *Ibid*, p. 372.
61. *Annals of Rural Bengal*, pages 19-30, 405, 415, Also see *Revenue chief of Bihar*, p. 5. Quoted in *Guide to the Records in the National Archives of India,* New Delhi, 1977.
62. *A Guide to the India Office Records (1600-1858)* by William Foster, London, 1919, page 41.

63. *Ibid*, p. 44.
64. *Guide to the Records in the National Archives of India*, Part II, Home Department/Ministry Affairs (1748-1957), New Delhi, 1977, p. 59.
65. K.K. Datta (ed.), *Catalogue of Patna*, Commissioner's Records (1813-1853), Patna, 1963, Introduction, p. XVI11.
66. *Patna Commissioner's Record*, Vol. XI, 'Letters from the collector of Bihar to the Members of the Board of Revenue for the Central Province', 20th January 1824 to 29th December, 1824, and 5th January to 22nd October, 1825, pp: 302-315.
67. Buchanan, I, p. 1.
68. Askari and Ahmad (ed.), *CHB* Vol. II, Part II, Appendix IV, p. 588.
69. Referring to the wretched state of affairs in those days Clive wrote that "such a scene of anarchy, confusion, bribery, corruption and extortion was never to be seen or heard of in any country..." Similarly, in his letter to the Court of directors, dated 30th September, 1765, Verelst says that ...every spring of this government was smeared with corruption, that principles or rapacity and oppression universally prevailed, and that every sparks of sentiment and public spirit was lost and extinguished in the ordinate lust of unmerited wealth". See Verelst, View of Bengal, Appendix 1, p. 1.
70. K.K. Datta (ed.), *CHB*, Vol. III, Part I, Patna, 1976, p. 118.
71. At the beginning of the eighteenth century, Bengal Bihar and Orissa were the three separate subas (provinces). The three provinces came under the rule of a single subedar in 1733. See Anil Chandra Banerjee and Bimal Kanti Ghosh (ed.), *A Narrative of the Transactions in Bengal 1760-64*, Calcutta, 1976, Introduction, p. 1.
72. *Ibid*, Introduction, p. v.
73. Firminger, *Historical Introduction to the Bengal Portion of Fifth Report*, pp. Cliv-Clvi.
74. Though Clive's letter and the reply of Pitt definitely show that there was some sort of consideration by the company to go for Diwani right in 1758 itself. However, I have not come across any such evidence from Shah Alam's official records which in someway-or the other could corroborate to the above British accounts.
75. Anil Chandra Banerjee and Bimal Kanti Ghosh (ed.), *op. cit.*
76. *Ibid*. p. XIV.
77. Clive reached Calcutta on 3rd May, 1765, As cited in K.K. Datta (ed.) *CHB*, Vol. III, Part I, Patna, 1976, p. 118.
78. See Appendix I. Also see Mill, *History of British India*, 1858, Chap. III, p. 305, f.n.
79. Askari & Ahmad (ed.), *CHB*, Appendix IV, p. 589:
80. Buchanan, I
81. *Ibid*, p. 57.
82. *Ibid*, p. 72.
83. *Ibid*, p. 77.
84. *Ibid*, p. 80.
85. *Ibid*, p. 84.
86. *Ibid*, p. 57.
87. *Ibid*, p. 57.

88. *Ibid*, p. 59. Also see K.K. Datta (ed.), *Catalogue of Patna Commissioner's Records (1813)*, Patna, 1 963, pp. XV-XIX.
89. Buchanan, I, pp. 59-60.
90. *Annals of Rural Bengal*, p. 405.
91. *Ibid*, pp. 38-39.
92. O'Malley, *op. cit*, p. 38.
93. *Ibid*, p. 41.
94. The village maliks are the survival from the revenue system of Mughal times. They were entitled to a proportion of the collections of rent made by the zamindar, which was often compounded for a fixed annual payment or for certain rent-free land. See O'Malley, *op.cit*., fn, p. 41.
95. K.K. Datta (ed.) *CHB*, Vol. III, Part 1, Patna, 1976, p. 1 .
96. Om Prakash, *The Dutch East India Company and the Economy of Bengal (1630-1720)*, Princeton, 1985, p.38.
97. *Ibid*, p.39.
98. Askari & Ahmad (ed.), *op. cit.*, p. 597.
99. S. Bhattacharya, *The East India Company and the Economy of Bengal*, London, 1954, p. 80.
100. Letter from Verelst to Court, seventeenth March 1767, *Fort William India House Correspondence*, Vol. V. p. 303.
101. N.L. Chatterjee's article Anglo-Dutch disputes in Bengal in *Proceedings, of Indian History Congress*, 1939, pp. 438-39.
102. K.K. Datta (ed.), *CHB*, Vol. III, Part I, p. 29.
103. *Ibid*, p. 29.
104. Bisheswar Porasad (ed.), Public Letter from Court, 23rd March 1770, Para 50, *Fort William India House Correspondence*.
105. Ibid, p. XXX.
106. Askari & Ahmad (ed.), *op. cit.*, p. 202.
107. S. Bhattacharya, *op. cit.*, p. 82.
108. Askari & Ahmad (ed.), *op.cit.*, p. 602.
109. K.K. Datta, *Selection from Unpublished Correspondence of the Judge*, p. 6 *Magistrate and the Judges of Patna*, p. 46.
110. S. Bhattacharya, *op. cit.*, p. 83.
111. cf. *Ibid*, p. 85.
112. Askari & Ahmad (ed.) *op. cit.*, p. 597.
113. *Ibid*, p. 598.
114. H.N. Sinha (ed.) *Fort William India House Correspondence, Vol. II (1764-66)*, National Archives of India, Delhi, 1962.

2

PRE-INDUSTRIAL TECHNOLOGY AND CRAFTSMANSHIP IN EIGHTEENTH CENTURY BIHAR

The artisans constituted a substantial section of population in few important cities of Bihar e.g. Patna, Purnea, Bhagalpur and Munghyr. They were involved in the manufacturing of items like textile, leather, sugar, salt, stone-work etc. Consequently these cities developed as important centres of commercial activities with the products of the artisans occupying the place of the pride. Many Europeans on behalf of their companies settled in these areas during the seventeenth and the eighteenth centuries and used to export artisanal products to Europe. Thus, prior to the establishment of modern industries the organisation of production remained in the hands of traditional craftsmen. However, there is no denying the fact that the English and the Dutch were able to affect the earlier trade-network during the second half of the eighteenth century and after. Therefore, how changes were made in the organisation of production after the East India Company got the diwani of Bengal in 1765 is an altogether different issue and would be taken up in the subsequent chapter.[1] Here we are only concerned with the pre-industrial technology brought into use by the indigenous artisans during the eighteenth century and how they organised the production on domestic basis.

Of the ninety-five crafts, cotton and silk industries were the oldest and were organised on a domestic basis. Almost every village had persons either engaged in spinning or weaving and many were involved in production of raw cotton and silk. The diagram given on next page shows the percentage involvement of artisans in textile industry. Cloth manufacture was quite flourishing in Patna in the early eighteenth century. Buchanan says, "cotton is by far the most common material used in cloth manufacture of these districts; and a great part of what is used is the produce of the country."

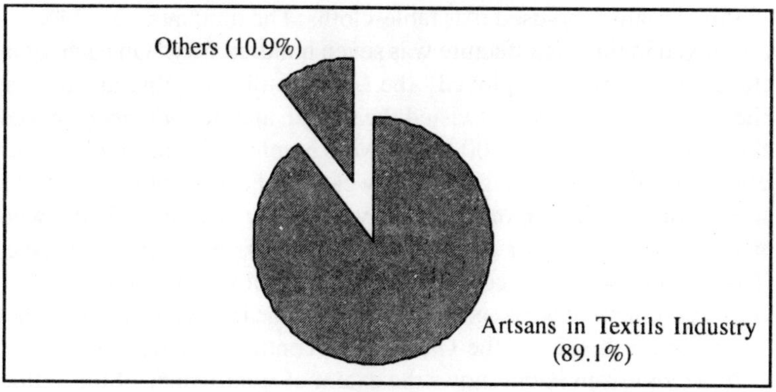

Fig. 2.1 : Involvement of Artisans in Textiles and Other Industries (1811-12)

Textile Workers

The earliest detailed account of crafts and craftsmanship in Bihar is found in the accounts of FrancisBuchanan, who took the monumental survey of this region in the early nineteenth Century. The artisans listed by Buchanan can be classified under three heads :

1. Those attached to the needs of the upper classes i.e. luxury oriented crafts;
2. Those who produced essential items needed by all; and
3. Those who produced items of common man's use. The artisans under these categories are tabulated in Appendix II.

Prior to the establishment of the modern industries the production of artisanal goods was organised on domestic basis. Cotton and silk industries were the oldest. Almost 90% of the artisans in Bihar were involved in textile industry. And among the textile workers, cotton was the most common material used.[2]

A majority of cotton weavers were involved in the production of coarse cloths which was used by the masses in general. However, there were many other weavers who manufactured finer cloths "for exportation, the company having had three factories dependent on Patna, and five subordinates to the other three, while native traders have established 22 houses for purchase of cloth".[3] The cotton weavers of Phatuha were employed in weaving cotton diaper *(khes),* which the natives used as a dress and much of this manufacture was sold to the Europeans who used it as table-cloths. The total number of looms employed in this manufacture was seven hundred fifty.[4] On each loom three persons were employed - the *Lungri* pulled the threads to form the pattern, the *Dobarah* twisted the thread, and the *Binkurui* weaved the cloth. In Purnea, 13500 looms were employed in producing finer and coarse good.[5] In Bhagalpur the weavers of cotton cloth were 6213 houses having 7279 looms[6]. There were many artisans at Patna who made *Chintz*[7] cloth for export. The *Newargars* weaved cotton tape. The production of raw cotton in Patna was not significant as most of the requirement of weavers was fulfilled by the import of cotton thread from the north side of the Ganges.[8] In contrast, the huge export of cotton cloth from Patna shows the extent of significance of the cotton cloth manufactured here. The total amount of export estimated by Buchanan was more than Rs. 5,45,000. Importantly, almost whole of it was sent to Calcutta and from there to Europe. "Some of that purchased by individuals is for the markets in the Gulph (Gulf) of Persia, and some is purchased by the Americans and the Portuguese."[9] R. Orme says that cloth being the staple manufacture of ideal trade in general is better encouraged here than in other despotic states because cloth happened to be one of the great resources of public revenue.[10]

Manufacturing cotton goods was a complex process.[11] After the collection of cotton crop from the field, the seeds were cleared from cotton. But this cotton remained full of dirt and knots and so to get rid of these it was ginned. The ginners *(dhuniya)* used a piece of bamboo stretched into a curve and joined together by means of leather string called *tant*.[12] Baines has described this apparatus as a large bow made elastic by a complication of strips. This was put in contact with a heap of cotton and the ginner strikes the strings with a heavy wooden mallet, the vibration open the knots of the cotton, shake off the dirt and raise it to a downy fleece.[13] The ginners in Patna constituted a distinct functional class.[14] Buchanan reports that one-third of the ginners of Patna had capital enough to enable them to buy a little cotton which they cleared and then retailed and the rest of the ginners worked entirely for hire.[15] He further says that a man and his wife could thus make Rupees three to four a month.[16]

Raw cotton was then spunned for obtaining yarn. Almost every house in the villages used to have its spinning wheel.[17] Since spinning was comparatively a lighter and less technical job it was quite often done by women. Buchanan informs that the work of separating the cotton from its seed and then spinning the yarn was mostly done by women. Nearly 3,30,426 women were engaged in Patna in one way or the other. MartinMontgomery has mentioned that in Bhagalpur 1,60,000 women were employed in spinning. A majority of these women spun only a few hours in the afternoon and there were many others who spun for longer hours.[18] The spinning equipment consisted of two types - one a spindle for finer yarns and two the spinning wheel used for coarse yarns. The spindle was made of metal or wood, which was turned around with left hand and the cotton was feeded with the right.[19] The coarse yarn was spun on a thread wheel of teakwood, which was turned by hand.[20] Buchanan says that the thread in Patna was spun on the small wheel common in India.[21] Forbes gives full detail about this spinning wheel—"The operators of the Indian wheel sat on the ground alongside the wheel. Some fibres of the carded silver are taken with left hand attached to the end of the spindle, which is then revolved by turning the driving wheel with the right hand. As the left hand holds the thread, feeding it with more fibres until the hand is at about three feet distance from the spindle, the fibres glide off the spindle at each turn and thus the turning of the spinning wheel transmits a twist to the stretched thread held at an oblique angle to the spindle. When a full arm length of thread has been spun the spinner stops the wheel, and, gliding it at right angles to the spindle, winds it up slowly by spinning the wheel in a contrary direction"[22].

According to Buchanan, the total output of yarn at Patna was worth Rs. 23,67,277 and the total margin of profit realised amounted to Rs. 10,81,005. He further says that at Patna during Vansittart's period as the Custom Master, the import duty calculations showed that the average annual import of cotton was valued at Rs. 3,50,000, which represented 35,000 mun (the British preferred to call it mun which is same as mun and equals 40kg.) of cotton at the rate of Rupees ten per mun. Deducting 1000 mun, used for stuffing purposes, the remaining 34,000 mun had been spun on the small wheel common in India.[23]

After spinning, the yarn was ready for weaving purposes and different types of cloths were weaved accordingly. Sometimes the yarn used to be starched prior to weaving to facilitate the weaving process.[24] The loom which was used for weaving was of imperfect structure usual in India.[25] "It consisted of two bamboo rollers serving for both the warp and weft. A single shuttle, also performing the job of batten, was made like a large netting needle and a pair of paddles completed the weaving requirements.[26] Buchanan reports that in the loom employed for weaving, the warp was stretched out the whole length and breadth of the piece intended to be wrought. The woof was not thrown across with a shuttle, but was passed through by several workmen, who brought the threads close together with wooden combs in place of a reed. The narrowest piece required two men, and 8 or 10 were often employed at this awkard labour.[27]

After weaving, the cloth was sent to the bleachers and then to the dyers. The bleachers used lime and some other local ingredients to boil their cloth, took it to a nearby river or pond, beat it vigorously on a stone slab with a beetle.[28]

Similar to the production of raw cotton, *cocoon*[29] (the egg-shape shell in which the silkworm put themselves) from which silk thread is obtained, too was very meagre and the required raw silk came from Kasimbazar, Ramgarh and Virbhum. According to Buchanan, the *Tasarguti* or *cocoons* of the *Tsar* silk were vastly underrated, the quantity required for the manufacture at the retail price being worth 1,89,000 rupees, and that produced in the country being trifling.[30] The weavers who made cloth of *Tsar* (silk) were confined to Phatuha, Gaya and Nawada. At Phatuha four qualities of siik cloth were produced - *Banusa, Maghaiyas, Lunggi* and *Sela,* all of which were used as wrappers and petticoats for women. *Sela* type was also produced at Gaya. But the speciality of the area was *Manpuridhuti,* which was wholely sold to the pilgrims. The Nawada silk cloth was called simply *Dhuti.*[31] Bhagalpur was famous for the manufacture of mixed fabrics of cotton and silk. There were 3275 looms engaged in its production. The famous varieties found in Bhagalpur were *Duriyas, Namunahs, Chaharkhanhs, baftahs* and *Khariasari.* Purnea district too was famous for mixed fabrics with about 7000 looms. However, at the same time there were about 125 houses having 200 looms in Purnea which exclusively produced cloths of pure silk.

The total number of looms in Patna was 1,622 out of which Phatuha alone had 1250 looms.[32] Each loom required one man and woman. Women generally did the work of winding and assisted in warping and dying the cloth.[33]

Closely related to the textile industry were a class of dyers, who were of four types - *Rungrej, Nelgur, Achfurosh* and *Gulalsaz.* The first dye various colours, the second dye with indigo alone, the third with the root of the Morinda alone, and the fourth with lac alone.[34] People who used to bleach cloth were called *Kundigars.*[35] Along with them worked a class of artists called *Parchahkush,*[36] who put all the threads in the bleached cloth at equal distances with the help of wooden comb. The *Kangnigars*[37] used to do ornamentation at the end of the pieces of cloth with the flattened gold and silver wire called *Badla.* It was not woven into the cloth but put in with a needle. Buchanan says that *Badla* was made at Patna and was of very good quality. *Buta banwaiyas*[38] were the women who flowered the cloth. The *Chhapagars*[39] put gold and silver flowers on fine muslin by the cloth in the form wished, with common glue, and then by applying gold and silver leaf which adhered to the glue, and rubbing off where that had not been applied. However, Buchanan says that this type of cloth could not be washed, but was very showy, and was used on high occasions.

Carpet weaving was another highly rated industry in Patna district. The carpet weavers produced three kinds of carpets here. One was *Shatranji* made entirely of cotton. The second kind was a mixture of wool and cotton. The base of the third was made of cotton and the woolen part was neatly piled over the cotton warp and woof. Buchanan, however, believes that the best of these carpet weavers were originally from Delhi. He reports that the carpet-makers of Daudnagar, originally from Delhi, were most skilful, and seemed to be in easy circumstances, and in one shop he found sixteen men weaving besides dyers and spinners[40]. Praising the quality, he says that these carpets were very handsome, and the workmen put in the pile with great dexterity, and formed the flowers very neatly without looking at a pattern. Another kind of weavers were the *Tashbaf,*[41] who weaved cloth of gold or silver and the *Gotasaz,* who made gold and silver laces.[42]

Leather Workers

Leather industry though scattered, held in its fold a large number of artisans who produced for the domestic market. Tanning of leather and other preparatory processes for converting hide into leather has also been described by Buchanan[43] in his *Patna - Gaya Report.* H.G. Walton[44] too has given details of similar tanning technique followed in India before the establishment of modern tanneries.

Leather was manufactured with the hides of various animals like buffalo, bullock, cow, goat, sheep, ass etc. There were two sources of raw hides - one from the dead animals and the other from the slaughtered animals. The animals which died in the villages were taken away by the *chamars.* At times, they were paid for removing the dead animals, otherwise the hides collected from the dead animals itself was considered to be their service charges. The people who tanned the hides of sheep and goat were the *chiks* (one of the types). They used to collect the hides of the two types of animals from various slaughter-houses and put them in processing. Not surprisingly, their position in the society was higher than those of the collectors of hides of other dead animals.

The preparation of hides took almost a month[45]. Before it could be brought to use for•product manufacturing, it went through three stages. In the first stage, the hairs from the raw skin was removed. In the second stage, the skin was put in liquor made of various local herbs and vegetations for processing. The final stage was that of drying the skin in the sun. To start with, the hides were soaked, split into sides and limed. These were left in pits with lime and soda from six to eight, or from twelve to fourteen days according to seasonal variations. The skins were then removed and unpaired with a *khurpi* or scraper and placed in a new lime solution without soda. When the skins were sufficiently swollen they were taken out and fleshed on a stone slab with a knife. They were then laid in clean water from four to six hours. The skin was again put into a solution consisting of tan liquor kept in an earthern vessel and was allowed to ferment for about a week. A second bathing was done in a solution of water mixed with molasses and *mahua* flour or with *mahua* refuse from a distillery. A third bathing was then made in a solution same as first, except that scraps of fleshing were used in the place of rice husks. However, H.G. Walton says that the third bathing was often neglected by the *chamars.* The hide was now laid on a slab, scrapped on the grained side and wrung dry. Again it was laid in strong tan liquor for twelve to twenty-four hours, being kneaded and wrung by hand at frequent intervals. If *pur* (a large leather bag used for water lifting from wells from irrigation) was to be made then the leather was sewed up with *moonj* (a grass) into a bag, hung up filled with tan mixture. This consisted of fifteen seers of new and ten seers of half-spent tan bark *(babool),* water and tan liquor. The bag was suspended by the neck from a wooden tripod over a *nad* (a large earthen vessel). As the liquor dripped through the holes it was poured back into the bag. After twenty-four hours the bag was taken down, the neck was sewn up and the bag was hung up reversed for twelve hours. The hide was then taken down, opened and laid out. It was sprinkled with four ounces of impure salt and four ounces of bark dust, which was then well ruffed in. Thus, leather bag was ready for use.

Another frequently used process by the household manufacturer of leather was liming[46]. The hides were laid on the floor and roughly flushed, smeared over with lime paste and folded up. The hide was then tied at both ends and placed in a *nad* containing lime solution. After three days the hide was removed unfolded and rubbed with lime. It was taken out, rubbed, scrapped, cleaned and washed with clean water. After the removal of the hair and flesh completely, the hide was fit for tanning. The hide, which became white, was soaked in clean water. In it a handful of bark was added and allowed to lie for two nights. The hide was then folded lengthwise and twisted until all the moisture was squeezed out. It was then unfolded, wet and twisted in the reverse way. The process of wetting and squeezing took the place of bathing[47]. The hide was then treated with tanin materials (as discussed in the earlier process). After this tanning process, the leather was curried with salt, curds, ghee and this completed the process.

G.W. Briggs feels that owing to the excessive use of lime the leather produced by the *chamars* was very porous and of inferior quality. The tanning was scarcely more than a colouring process. The object of tanning was to produce, by a combination of tanin with the gelatine of the hide or skin, an insoluble impenetrable substance. The lime destroyed to a considerable extent the fibres upon which the tanin acts.[48]

To make the leather coloured, special processes were followed. Briggs[49] says that to produce red leather *has* was put into the gruel bath. Blue leather was obtained by the use of copper filings, sal ammonia and lime juice; and black leather by the use of copper. Sal was used to give rich brown colour, *dhadra* to give light yellow. The combination of these materials produced different shades of colour[50].

The *kimokhtsaz*[51] prepared leather from the skins of horses and asses. It was only the skin of the hinder parts that was used. This was put for four days in water, and then the hair was removed by scraping. Then flesh side of the skin was covered with the small millet called *China,* which was pressed into the skin. It was then dried in the sun, and the hair-side was scrapped five times. The skin was then dipped in water, after which the flesh-side was again scrapped, and the leather was boiled in a solution of the salt called *bherkhari.* The flesh-side was then covered with copper filings and sal ammonia, and then with a layer of grass. Above this were laid eight or ten hides, one above the other and the whole was pressed by a weight. In eight days the skin were found of a fine green colour, and were fit for use.

The *Dabgars*.[52] made leather bags for holding *ghee* (butter), oil and thin extract of sugarcane. They also made targets of the hides of buffaloes. The bags used to be of two sizes - the larger made of the hides of buffaloes, the smaller of those of oxen.

Interestingly, in the absence of any chemical for the process of tanning, these traditional leather-workers used local herbs and vegetations as a substance for tanning, the list of which along with their botanical name is given below (Table 2.1)[53]

Table 2.1 : List of Herbs Used for Tanning

Substance	*Botanical Name*
1. Bark and leaves of *Babool* tree	*Acacia Arabica*
2. *Dhadra or Bakli*	*Anogeissus Latifolia*
3. Bark of *Sal*	*Shoria Robusta*
4. *Har*	*Terminalia Chebula*
5. *Bahaira*	*Terminalia Bellerica*
6. *Bamda*	*A parasite commonly found on the mango tree*
7. *Aonla*	*Phyllanthus Embhica*
8. Bark of Amaltas	*Cassia Fistula*
9. Bark of Rhea	*Acacia Leucophlarea*
10. Bark of Avaram	*Cassia Auriculata*
11. *Kharwa*	*Vateria Indica*

Source : G.W. Briggs, *The Chamars,* appendix, p. *259.*

Leather industry though scattered, held in its fold a large number of artisans who produced largely for the domestic market[54]. These tanners of leather, the prepares of skin, the manufacturers of leather article, and the makers of shoes belonged to an occupational group called *Chamar*[55]. It is as a tanner, a skilled worked in leather that the *chamar* obtains his name. About the *chamars,* Buchanan says that in the country parts they were chiefly employed to make coarse shoes leather ropes and drum heads, which they beat with great diligence[56]. But, a catalogue of the different kinds of work which the *chamar* perform, shows that he belonged to a class of unskilled labour. "He is a grass-cutter, coolie, wood and bundle-carrier, drudge, does off jobs, maker and repairer of thatch and of mudwalls, field-labour, groom, house-servant, peon, brick-maker, and even village watchman... Besides, he beats drums, rings bells and blows trumpets at wedding or when cholera or other epidemics are being exorcised from the village. He also makes musical instruments".[57]

Sometimes terms like *mochi* was also used to denote this class. Briggs says that *mochi is* a purely occupational off-shoot from the *chamar. Mochi* were divided into two main classes, those who made cobble shoes, who were real *chamars* and those who made saddle and harness. In some places the *mochi* of the town were divided into functional sub-castes, such as saddlers, embroiderers of saddle cloth, ghee-bucket makers, makers of spangles and of shields and scabbards.[58]

Table 2.2 : List of Various Types of Leather Workers in Patna District in 1811-12.

Type	*Function*	*Number*
Chik	Tanned sheep and goat skins	4
Kimokhtsaz	Prepared leather from ass and horse skins	3
Dabgar	Bag and target maker	32
Chamar	Tanners and shoe-makers	3462
Chikundoz	Made shoes of black cloth embroidered with coloured silk	02
Zurdoz	Made embroidered part of fine shoes	37
Kufsdoz	Joined embroidered part to the leather in fine shoes	6
Saddle-maker	Made saddle of leather (Name not given)	1
Khugirdoz	Made saddle cloth	10
Whip-maker	Made whips called chabuks (Name not given)	4

Source : Francis Buchanan, *An Account of Districts of Bihar and Patna,* pp.767-68.

There are certain close-up editary rights which were the privilege of a certain *chamar* family (ies) in each village[59]. These rights, called *jajman* or *gaukarna* were carefully guarded. In return for these perquisites the *chamar* gave regular services to the landlords. The circle of clients from whom he received these privileges, expected him to remove dead cattle, prepare leather from the hide, and furnish a certain limited supply of shoes and other leather articles. However, Buchanan notes that the leather workers were paid chiefly in grain and belonged to a manorial establishment[60]. They were paid by a share of crop for finishing ropes, bags for drawing water and shoes for the ploughman[61].

The above description clearly shows that particular occupational castes tanned leather and produced leather article[62]. However, this does not necessarily mean that all the members of a particular caste were exclusively attached to the manufacturing of the specified product. Not more than 8% *chamars* in Bihar lived by working in leather, the remainder being cultivator[63]. In Shahabad, *chamars* were numerous and many did not work in their traditional occupations.[64] However, the people who actually did the tanning work, themselves had a social hierarchy within their group depending upon the nature of the dead animals they dealt in. Nevertheless, the people who prepared the leather were lower in hierarchy than those who worked in the leather after its preparation.

Sugar Manufacturers

The confectioners of Patna district were generally the preparers of *shukkur.* They did it by putting some thin extract of sugarcane into coarse sack cloth bags, and by putting a weight on these to squeeze out the molasses. Buchanan mentions that at Behar there were 15 houses of the Mahuri tribe, where refined sugar *(chini)* was made.[65] These people put 25 sers of the *shukkur* in a basket and laid some of the aquatic plant[66] on the surface to refine sugar. After three days about 2½ sers of refined sugar were scrapped from the surface and more plants were applied. This process was repeated until the whole *shukkur* got exhausted. According to the survey made by Buchanan of these tribal manufacturers of Behar, on an average eight sers of raw sugar and 17 sers of molasses were procured from 25 sers of *shukkur.* But this process of manufacturing was suitable only in the heats of spring. Most of this sugar produced was purchased by petty traders and was sold in the local market.

Another group of sugar manufacturers lived in Kelsa (Hilsa) region. There were about twenty such artisans in the area and were more wealthy men than those of Behar.[67] The process followed by the Hilsa sugar manufacturers was quite different from those of Behar, and they prepared their sugar by boiling. At first, *shukkur* was formed by extracting sugarcane in coarse bags of sack cloth. It was afterwards squeezed into bags of strong cotton cloth. The one mun (82 lbs.) of *shukkur* was then put into an earthen vessel with about 41 1bs. of water, and was boiled for about 30 minutes. Gradually 4 1bs. of milk and 8 1bs. of water was added and the liquid was left for boiling for three hours. It was then strained through a cotton cloth spread on a basket. The strained liquid called *sira* was again boiled for 30 minutes in small earthen vessels, each containing 4 to 6 1bs. The whole was then emptied into a large earthen cooler called a *nad* (a type of earthen pot), which had a hole in its bottom. The hole was plugged with a bamboo, which was pulled up after three days. Then the treacle was allowed to flow for two days. Subsequently, the aquatic plants were applied for cleaning the sugar.

The profit of the sugar manufacturers in a year varied for the two regions in Patna district. While the Behar manufacturers gained Rs. 137 in a season, the Hilsa boilers gained Rs. 148 in a season.[68] Thus, the condition of the Hilsa boilers was better than that of Behar.

Salt Manufacturers

The manufacture of saltpetre (or nitre) was carried on in abundance in Patna district.[69] Though the East India Company had by the middle of the eighteenth century established few factories all over the district with a chief factory at Patna town, the initial production of saltpetre was carried out by the indigenous manufacturers known as *Nuniyas,*[70] who collected saline earth from walls of the villages and turned it into crude saltpetre after boiling it. Crude saltpetre was purchased by the East India Company either after first boiling or sometimes after second boiling through the company agents.[71] Since the company gave low price to these indigenous manufacturers, Buchanan reports, they practiced every species of adulteration. The company, therefore, started buying crude saltpetre just after the first boiling and then refined it in its own factories through the use of copper. The company hired workers for the refining process. According to Buchanan, one man, one woman and two boys or girls, were usually employed at each furnace for six months.

The process of refining the crude saltpetre in English factories was simple, but the natives could not use the method because copper was totally beyond their reach.[72] About 15 muns (600 sers)·of crude saltpetre was put into a large copper vessel containing boiling water. When dissolved, the brine was taken out and poured into large earthen vessels. In these it was left for an hour to allow the earth to subside. The clear brine was then put into earthen pots (*nads*) where it remained for a day. The whole was then emptied into the copper, and boiled for about 2½ hours. To the hot liquid was added 30 muns of crude saltpetre, and after the earth subsided, the brine was put into *nads* where it remained for a day. Nearly 5 or 6 sers of finest saltpetre in crystallised form was thus obtained. It has been estimated that a hundred *muns* of crude saltpetre gave 60 *muns* of refined saltpetre.[73]

Glass Workers

The glass workers who blow and make glass were very few in Bihar. There was a class called *shishahgurs* who blew glasses and prepared glasswares for the Europeans.[74] Buchanan says that their work was rude because of the imperfection of their furnace. The glass was usually filled with air bubbles, waves and acquired greenish colour. But few literary works of the later period maintain that the glasswares of Patna district were of good quality. *Yadgar-e Rozgar* refers to Shaikh Mian Jaan Shishagar who made glasswares and sold them at exhibitions and obtained awards and certificate.[75] *Naqsh-e Paidar* too praises the glasswares of Patna.[76]

Another group of glass workers residing in Patna produced glass for those ornament workers who made ornaments of glass. They used to collect saline efflorescence (soda) from *Aghan* to *Magh* (from mid November to mid February) and put it into a cistern. The cistern was filled with water and was allowed to evaporate by the reaction of the air. It required 10 to 12 days to evaporate fully. When dry, at the bottom of the cistern a thick saline crust was obtained. This soda made glass without addition. As far as the condition of these glass manufacturers goes "they seem to be poor."[77]

Other Artisans

Other important artisan groups were those of indigo manufacturers[78], bricklayers called *puzayah, kumhars* (potters), *sungturash* (stone cutters). The *Kangjar* was a class of rope-makers who made ropes of grasses called *Sabe* and *Muj.* Buchanan says that most of the rope-makers were vagrants and used to travel through the country. The *Abirgars* were the one who made red starch used in Holi (a festival of colours). The starch prepared at Daudnagar was made from coarse grain, and was very inferior to that prepared from the root of the plant called *Tikhur.*[79] *Barhais* (Carpenters) were also a sizable population here. Patna and Dinapur were celebrated for their skilled carpenters whose dexterity is attested by the handsome carved balconies found in these towns. A large quantity of European furniture and other cabinet work of good quality was made at Dinapur and Patna and exported to other places.[80] *Naqsh-a Paidar* refers to the manufacture of exotic fire-works *(atishbazi)* and their public display on certain occasion[81] It gives a brief account of the kite-flying contests as well. This shows that kite-flying (*Guddi* or *Patang)* was a very popular game of amusement and, therefore, must have given employment to many kite-makers. Buchanan, however, observes that although many great idle fellows amused themselves with paper kites, the makers could not live the whole year by this profession as few amused themselves with this sport except in the cool season. The kite-makers, therefore, retailed toys for children, which were made by the potters, and the apparatus used in smoking tobacco.[82] Besides these there were many blacksmiths scattered in various parts of Bihar. Munghyr was most famous for manufacture of iron items after Eruopean fashion like fire-arms, tea-kettle, and dishes[83]. Biharsharif and Arwal were famous for manufacture of good quality of paper.[84] Daudnagar was famous for blanket weaving.[85]

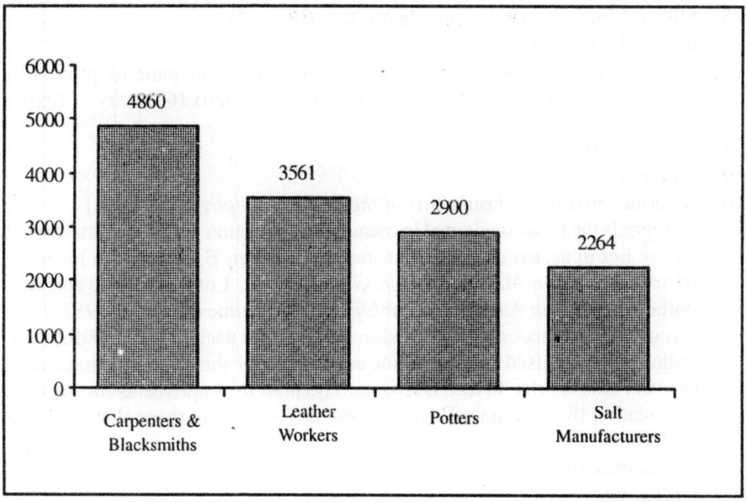

Fig. 2.2 : Distribution of Important Artisans Other than Textile (1811-12)

The crux of the discussion is that indigenous technology, though organised on domestic basis and smaller basis, had wide artisanal involvement. The artisans and craftsmen were both the workers as well as the owners of their own industries. Their involvement in the production process was bound to be maximum. It was because of this that the resultant quality production made them to capture large European market. The moment Europeans, specially the British deliberately started to intervene in the organisation of production, the pre-industrial technology became the thing of the past. The British manipulated the conditions of production and the existing relations to their own advantage resulting in the exploitation of indigenous artisans in the vield form and gradually in real terms after the establishment of modern industries.

NOTES

1. See Vipul Singh "Professional Mobility and Change : The World of Artisans in late Eighteenth Century Patna" in *Studies in History and Culture,* Vol. 4, No. 2, Sept. 1996.
2. Francis Buchanan, *An Account of Districts of Bihar and Patna in 1811-12,* Vol. II, p.647.
3. *Ibid*, p. 652.
4. *Ibid*, p. 652.
5. Martin Montgomery, *Eastern India, Vol. III,* p. 328.
6. *Ibid*, Vol. II, p. 276.
7. *Chintz* was a type of cotton cloth with floral or other patterns printed or painted. See Irfan Habib's *Atlas,* Delhi, 1986, Appendix (Glossary of Textile Terms).
8. Buchanan II, p. 676.
9. Ibid; p. 677.
10. R. Orme, *Historical Fragments of the Mughal Empire,* 1783, p. 411.
11. As regards the process adopted in manufacturing cotton goods in Patna district we are not in access of detailed material. However, E.J. Baines in his book *History of Cotton Manufacture in Great Britain,* London, 1835, and R.J. Forbes, *Studies in Ancient Technology,* Four Volumes, Leiden, 1957, have given a detailed account of the traditional methods used in cotton industry in India. We have used their account assuming that the same methods were used in Patna district. In fact, Buchanan says that "the implements for cleaning and beating the cotton (in Patna) are not different from those that are usual (in India)." See p. 649.
12. E.J. Baines, *op. cit.,* p. 67.
13. *Ibid*, p. 67.
14. Buchanan, II, p. 647.
15. *Ibid*, p. 647.
16. *Ibid*, p. 647.
17. J.C. Ray, 'Textile Industry in Ancient India' , *JBORS*, Vol. III, Part III, p. 222.
18. Buchanan, II, p. 647.
19. E.J. Baines, *op. cit.*, p. 68.
20. *Ibid*, p. 68.
21. Buchanan, II, p. 649.
22. R.J. Forbes, *Studies in Ancient Technology,* Vol. IV, Leiden, 1957, p. 156.
23. Buchanan, II, p. 647.
24. *Ibid*, p. 653.

25. *Ibid*, p. 653.
26. E.J. Baines, *op. cit.*, p. 69.
27. Buchanan, II, p. 656.
28. *Ibid*, p. 654.
29. Cocoon is called *Koya* in Patna district. *Ibid*, p. 651.
30. *Ibid*, p. 677.
31. *Ibid*, p. 651.
32. See Table No. 41, Ibid, p.772.
33. *Ibid*, p. 651.
34. *Ibid*, p. 649.
35. *Ibid*, p. 654.
36. *Ibid*, p. 654.
37. *Ibid*, p. 655.
38. *Ibid*, p. 655.
39. *Ibid*, p. 655.
40. *Ibid*, p. 656.
41. *Ibid*, p. 658.
42. *Ibid*, p. 658.
43. *Ibid*, pp. 626-27.
44. H.G. Walton, *A Monograph on Tanning and Working in Leather,* 1903.
45. G.W. Briggs, *The Chamars,* Delhi, 1920, p. 256.
46. *Ibid*, p. 256.
47. *Ibid*, p. 258.
48. *Ibid*, p. 258.
49. *Ibid*, p. 258.
50. *Ibid*, p. 259.
51. Buchanan, II, p. 626.
52. *Ibid*, p. 626-27.
53. Briggs, *op.cit.*, appendix, p. 259.
54. Buchanan, II, *op.cit.*, p. 627.
55. Bruggs, *op. cit.*, p.11.
56. Buchanan, II, *op.cit.*, p.627.
57. Briggs, *op.cit,* p. 56.
58. *Ibid*, pp. 33-34.
59. T. Morrison, *Industrial Organisation of an Indian Province,* 1906, pp. 179-80.
60. *Buchanan's Report on Bhagalpur District in 1810-11,* Vol. V., p. 16.
61. *Buchanan's Report on Shahabad District in 1812-13,* Vol. V., pp. 13-14.
62. Vipul Singh, *The Artisans of Patna District between. 1765 & 811,* unpublished M.Phil. Dissertation, Delhi University, Delhi, 1996, pp.46-48.
63. Sir H.H. Risley, *People of India,* 1908, pp. 76-77.
64. *Buchanan's Report on Shahabad District, op. cit.* pp.13-14.
65. *Ibid*, p. 659.
66. Some of these plants mentioned by Buchanan are, Valisneria spiralis, Serpicula Verticillata and Potomogetons. See *Ibid*, pp. 659-660.
67. *Ibid*, p. 660.
68. *Ibid*, pp. 660-61.
69. *Letter from J. Wintle, Magistrate of Bhagalpur to T. Brown, Commercial*

Resident at Patna, dated the seventeenth October 1803, Bhagalpur District Records.

70. . Journal *of Indian History,* April 1941, Supplement, p. 14.
71. Buchanan, II, p. 665.
72. *Ibld*, p. 665.
73. *Ibid*, p. 666.
74. Buchanan,II, p. 620.
75. Syed Badrul Hasan, *Yadgar-e-Rozgar,* Patna City, 1931, pp. 72-74.
76. Ali Muhammad Shad, *Naqsh-e-Paidar,* Patna City, 1924, p. 213.
77. Buchanan, II, p. 621.
78. Bihar happened to be one of the main indigo manufacturing regions of India during the end of eighteenth and early nineteenth centuries with the factories mainly established in the districts of Saran, Tirhut, Purnea and Bhagalpur. Patna district could not emerge as an important indigo manufacturing centre. There were only seven indigo factories at the time of Buchanan's survey in Patna district. See Buchanan, II, Table No. 41, p. 773. (Buchanan does not give any detailed account of indigo manufacturers in Patna district). One of the reasons why indigo industry could not grow here was because the zamindars in general were much averse to indigo plantation. See K.K. Datta (ed.) *Comprehensive History of Bihar,* Vol. III, Part I, p. 462. Buchanan says that Raja Mitrajit Singh of Tikari had expelled it (indigo cultivation) entirely from his estate. As a matter of fact several factories had been totally abandoned and the remaining seven were far from thriving. See Buchanan, II, p. 527.
79. *Ibid*, p. 619.
80. cf. Surendra Gopal, *Patna in the Nineteenth Century,* Calcutta, 1982, p. 50.
81. Ali Muhammad Shad, *op.cit.,* p.215.
82. Buchanan, II, p.625.
83. Martin, *Eastern India,* Vol. II, p. 266.
84. Buchanan, Vol. II, pp. 616-17.
85. *Ibid*, p. 657.

3

PROFESSIONAL MOBILITY AND ORGANISATION OF PRODUCTION

Eighteenth century India saw the decline of Mughal centralized state[1] and consequently a weakening of the ruling elites. During the sixteenth and seventeenth centuries these elites had provided patronage to arts and crafts, but their decline also meant the fall in the demand of these specialised products. However, there were a number of other artisanal products manufactured at various regional centres which had nothing to do with the demands of these elites e.g. textile, sugar, leather goods, salt, etc. So the question arises as to whether the fall of the empire signify stoppage or even a reversal of the processes of economic development of the seventeenth century? Or, did the process continue in a different manner? Dharma Kumar[2] feels that continuity was the main feature of the economic life of India during the eighteenth century. C.A. Bayly,[3] endorsed by Muzaffar Alam,[4] too puts forward the hypothesis that the early British rule was a continuation of the preceding Indian regimes. But we should not overlook the impact of the European trading activities, which Steensgaard has also accepted. He says that. the English and the Dutch were able to affect the earlier trade network.[5] As a deliberate colonial policy, the English used their power to alter the conditions of production and the existing relationships between the artisans and themselves. Patna (presently capital of Bihar), being an important production centre and a trading point could not escape the wrath of colonial exploitation during the second half of the eighteenth century. Here it is worth mentioning the idea put forward by Irfan Habib. He would like the historians to separate the eighteenth century into two parts and then study the economic implications of the colonial rule.[6] Athar Ali also feels that to lump the pre-colonial and colonial phases together in a single century, is difficult to comprehend, unless one refuses to consider the colonial conquest as a fundamental break at all.[7] Satish Chandra calls this second half as a 'grey period' in India's economic history, during which British control over India's trade and internal economy steadily expanded and ultimately reduced India to the position of a colony exporting raw materials to Britain and importing manufactured goods.[8] However, at the same time he believes that the handicraft production of India did not suffer any sharp decline during this period.[9] But the process in this direction had actually started with the change in the organization of production.[10] This is what the present chapter has tried to delve into, taking Patna as a case study.

The total population of artisans in Patna district was nearly 4,64,500.[11] We have estimates for the pre-census population of various townships and capital cities, but these estimates are sometimes very vague and based on neither logic nor any reason. While we are fortunate in having the population of Patna district for the year 1811-12 based on Buchanan's actual house count, we can arrive at the percentage/ratio of the artisans and agricultural labours in relation to the total population. The following table gives us an idea:

Table 3.1 : Population Distribution

A	*B*	*C*	*D*	*E*
Total popula-tion	*Artisans' popula-tion*	*Agriculture population*	*Percentage of B as compared to A*	*Percentage of C as compared to A*
33,64.420	4,64,500	20,94,100	13.8%	62.2%

Source : Francis Buchanan, *An Account of the Districts of Bihar and Patna in 1811 12.* Table No. 4. p. 723.

We find that the percentage of the agriculturists is higher than the population of the artisans in Patna district. This is obviously because many of the professional groups of artisans were involved in the agriculture sector and for them working for their profession was often a side job. As we will see that only 8 per cent of the total population of the *Chamars* were involved in their profession while the rest were attached to agriculture.

Professional Mobility and the Caste

A very interesting aspect of the artisans in general was their caste ties. Weaving was generally confined to a particular caste among the Hindus, namely the *Tatwa* and a particular section of the

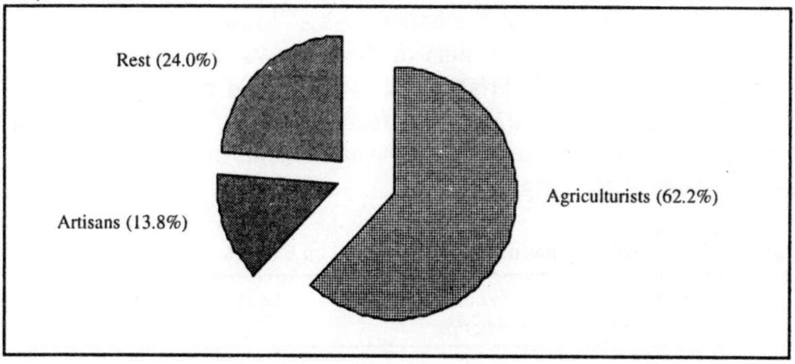

Fig. 3.1 : Percentage Distribution of Population in Patna District (1811-12)

Muhammedans called *Julaha.*[12] Particular varieties of textiles came to be produced by particular sub-caste and virtually every operation connected with the production of cloth-cotton-carding, spinning, winding silk-thread, unwinding and rewinding the yarn, formation of the cloth on the loom, bleaching, dyeing, printing and painting of designs - developed into distinct occupations, some came to be associated with exclusive caste categories.[13] Similarly, other professionals like blanket-weavers, tailors, washermen, blacksmiths, carpenters, cotton cleaners, potters, ornament makers, leather workers, lac workers etc. were also attached to a particular caste either among the Hindus or the Muslims, the list of which is given ahead in table 3.2.

The so-called *Jajmani* system was the characteristic basis for rural manufacturing organisation. "Hereditary professional artisans were maintained collectively by the village community which allocated to them a certain share, rigidly fixed by tradition, of peasants' crops in kind and sometimes also a small plot of land. In return the artisans supplied the members of their community with their products."[14] But this is only true for occupational groups like oilpressers, carpenters, blacksmiths, leather workers etc. who combined their production for market with their customary service obligation to the village community. A number of other artisanal groups sold their products directly in the market and were not tied to the village community. There were many carpenters and blacksmiths who produced for the local market and many others who lived in villages and exclusively worked and produced for the villagers. Thus, there was a clear differentiation between artisans catering for the market and those tied to the village community. Buchanan says - "In the country they pay no house rent and receive most of their allowances in grain which valued at harvest price, produced a low nominal reward, but keeps them in plenty of food... They usually belong to the manorial establishment, and the payment for the implements of agriculture arises from a share of the crop."[15]

Table 3.2 : List of Occupational Groups Based on Caste

	Profession	*Whether Hindu or Muslim*	*Traditional Caste*
1.	Weavers of cloth	Both	*Jolaha, Banaudhiya*
2.	Blanket weavers	Information not available.	*Garrariya*
3.	Tailors	Mostly Muslims, few Hindus.	*Darji*
4.	Washermen (who bleach cloth)	Both	*Dhobi*
5.	Blacksmith	Hindu	*Lohar*
6.	Carpenter	Hindu	*Badhai*
7.	Cotton beaters and cleaners	Muslim	*Dhuniya*
8.	Potters	Both	*Kumhar*
9.	Ornament makers[16]	Hindu	*Sonar*
10.	Lac workers	Hindu	*Laheri or Nari*
11.	Leather workers	Both	*Muchi, Chamar, Chic etc.*

Source : Francis Buchanan, *An Account of Districts of Bihar and Patna in* 1811-1812, Passim.

It is evident from the above table, that a few occupational castes produced a particular product, but this does not necessarily mean that all members of a particular caste were exclusively attached to the manufacture of the specified product. There are numerous references to intersectional mobility on horizontal level.[17] Buchanan has given an account of the mass of ordinary and unskilled people who took to or were engaged in the production process to be included in a new class of skilled professions. *Kasera* of Patna district who made vessels of copper, brass and bellmetal employed many such workers.[18] This process of mobility of the artisans was further enhanced with the coming of the British and establishment of the factories at Patna. They needed a large number of artisans to work in the factories and they were not necessarily of a particular occupational caste. For example, to refine saltpetre at Patna factory, workers were hired who were often unskilled.[19] There are also instances within the local occupational groups where a particular product was being produced by different castes and tribes. Sugar was manufactured both by Mahuri tribe at Bihar and by different confectioners (not a caste) at Dinapur and Patna town.[20] Another evidence of such intersectional mobility can be discerned from the following statement of Buchanan. "Many of these (artisans) have not only farms, but hold the plough or labour the earth with their own hands, and either cultivate the ground. when they do not find employment at their trade, or one brother cultivates the farm, while another follows the duties of his profession".[21] Even H.H. Risley, who wrote a century later, says that not more than 8 per cent of *Chamars* in Bihar live by working in leather, the remainder being cultivators.[22]

Closely related to the artisanal works is the question of introduction of technological devices. The state of the productive forces in the handicrafts was characterised by simple and primitive tools, but at the same time there was a fairly high degree of productive experience and craftsmanship.[23] According to Karl Marx "it is only the special skill accumulated from generation to generation and transmitted from father to son, that gives to the Hindu... this proficiency.[24] Similarly, Baines explains the remarkable fine sense of touch in terms of hereditary continuance of a particular species of manufacture in families through many generations.[25] In the process of manufacturing a piece of cloth, the labour and skill of the entire family, from head of the family to the little child, was considered useful. This is not only true for cotton weaving family but other artisans' family as well, as is clear from the accounts of Buchanan. Though Buchanan does not go into the details of the contribution of individual members of an artisan's family, but while explaining the average income of a particular class of artisans, he often calculates it in terms of 'family gain'.

When the demand far a particular product increased in Patna the traditional method of manufacturing was not given up. In fact, the extreme simplicity of instruments and a general indifference to labour - saving devices were perhaps the most characteristic features of India's manufacturing techniques.[26] Buchanan writes that. "...in India it is seldom that an attempt is made to accomplish anything by machinery that can be performed by human labour."[27] But, then how did the artisans of Patna manage to expand their production with the continuance of the traditional methods of manufacturing and production? This was possible partly due to the change in the organisation of production with the coming of the British. The other factor contributing to the expansion of production with the increasing demand was the inclusion of outside elements in the family-based production. The master craftsmen (who were the heads of their family) moved out of their family and began to employ apprentices and servants by providing them necessary training in skills. For example, the *Kaseras* who made vessels of different metals in Patna had one master craftsman in each family. Buchanan says, "the chief man does nothing but melts the materials, forms the moulds, and cast .... The beating required by far the most dexterity, but the man who does it is usually hired and paid for the job."[28] These apprentices were paid small sums as wages.[29] About the brick-layers, Buchanan writes that common workmen are allowed from three to four rupees a month and principal artists often received double.[30] Further, if we look at the figures provided by Buchanan regarding the number of various artists in Patna district, the number of cotton weavers has not been given. What is given is the number of houses of cotton weavers and the number of looms. It is of significance in this regard that the number of looms is much more than the number of weaving families (See Table 3.3). This implies that production must have been carried on by small master weavers possessing two or three looms and employing usually one or more apprentices.

Table 3.3 : Number of Houses and Looms

Weavers	*No. of Houses*	*No. of Looms*
Cotton	19,900	24,352
Silk	782	1,622

Source : Francis Buchanan. *An Account of Districts of Bihar and Patna in* (1811-12) Table 41, p. 772.

Organisation of Production

The traditional organization of production gradually changed with the growth of European commerce. The Dutch had already entered Patna and by the 1760s the English too had established factories at Patna. To procure commodities, the company advanced money to the '*dadni*'[31] merchants. Buchanan has given a few references to the system of advances, though by that time this system had seized to exist. The basic reason of *dadni* was the inadequacy of capital available to the artisans for the requirements of an expanded and expanding market. Secondly, *dadni* gave the artisans the necessary security as there was always a risk of heavy losses if the European companies rejected their products.

The East India Company abandoned the method of procuring investment through *dadni* merchants in 1753.[32] The English found it cheaper to discontinue cash advances to weavers, and instead to buy the silk raw and then give it out to the weavers. The reason for this was said to be that the latter, out of poverty, could not buy raw silk of the requisite quality even when granted advances.[33] Under the newly adopted method, the company engaged the weavers to work on a system of advances under which the weavers were bound to give their entire produce to the company. Buchanan has explained the prevalent practices in detail —"Each man on becoming bound *(Asami)* to the company received two rupees, and engaged not to work for any person until he had made as the company required; and no other advance has ever been made by the commercial residents. The agent orders each man to make a certain number of pieces of such or such goods, and he is paid for each on its delivery, according to the price stated..."[34] Thus, the putting out system[35] was widely in use, as many would like us to believe.[36]

There is no denying the fact that many of these elements were common to the putting out system of late medieval and early modern Europe and the system of financing by merchants to the weavers practiced in European world. But while in Europe the goods produced belonged to the financier and the payment made to the producer consisted solely of the wages for his labour, in India the weaver appears to have retained his independence and his control over his produce, though his freedom to fix the price of his goods was not unrestricted. Often he only secured a money advance, not raw materials, had control over his tools and thus was master of the produced goods till they changed hands.[37]

About the Chintz makers at Patna, Buchanan says—"The tradesmen of Patna make Chintz for exportation, and use new cloth. Some of them have a little capital, find the materials and servants, and print the cloth at so much a price for the merchants, who export it, but none can purchase the calico, print it, and stand the sale of Chintz. A great many, indeed, cannot find the apparatus, and work as mere servants to the merchant, who furnishes everything."[38]

However, with such a state of things, as the trade of the English East India Company increased, the oppression upon the weavers began to loom large. Often the weavers were forced to undertake the company's business and were trapped in the vicious cycle of 'balance and recovery'. Buchanan feels that the system pursued by the company was to keep the workmen in a state of dependence little better, if so good, as slavery.[39] According to Bolts, "the company's investment for Europe in a peculiar degree has been the one continued scene of oppression, the baneful effects of which are severely felt by every weaver and manufacturer in the country, every article produced being made a monopoly, in which the English with their Banyans and black *gomastas* (agents) arbitrarily decide what quantities of goods each manufacturer shall deliver and the prices he shall receive for them."[40] The artisans were unwilling to work for the company, since they were not paid a fair price for their labour. The oppressions went to such an extent that many of them gave up their profession. Verelst, in a letter to the Court of Directors (March 17, 1767) referred to the uncommon scarcity of weavers, a great number of whom had "deserted their profession to seek subsistence from a less precarious calling and hence follow those unavoidable disputes which so frequently happen with the French and the Dutch, who leave no means untried to reduce the weavers, from our service"[41]. It was observed that the weavers refused to take advances on account of the company as they found it more to their advantage to make cloths with the little money they had of their own and to bring it to the market, where they sold it to the Paikars employed both by the company and the individuals but chiefly to the latter as they got a higher price for their cloths.[42] In order to stop the desertation of the cotton weavers various regulations were provided by the company the details of which are given in Appendix III. The different regulations passed by the Government for the weavers were mainly aimed to make advances to the weavers before they receive advances from rival mercantile groups and to keep them in constant employment of the company. Compulsive regulations were passed from time to time during the last decades of the eighteenth century. The objective of the English Company was to become the sole purchaser of the goods produced by artisans catering to the European market. Apart from devising an elaborate machinery to enforce compulsive regulations, the company made use of outstanding balances against the artisans as the means of perpetuating their continued association with the company.

By the end of the eighteenth century, the British East India Company had been successful in fulfilling its need for export of different products such as saltpetre, cotton, sugar etc. The period had already witnessed some signs of professional mobility among the artisans and the British exploited this change to their own advantage. They manipulated the conditions of production and the existing relations resulting in the exploitation of indigenous artisans in the vield form. The exploiting tendencies were visible only after the oppression of artisans started in real terms.[43] Thus, in the larger context, the detrimental effect of colonial policy began as early as after 1765 after the company got the diwani of Bengal. The trend of expansion of industry was checked after 1765 by the establishment of the English monopoly over the trade and production of various goods at Patna.

NOTES

1. See Satish Chandra, *Parties and Politics at the Mughal Court, (1707-40), Aligarh,* 1959; p . XVII. Irfan Habib, *Agrarian System of Mughal India, 1556-1707,* Bombay, 1963: M. Athar Ali, *The Mughal Nobility under Aurangzeb,* OUP, 1997.
2. Dharma Kumar (ed .), *Cambridge Economic History of India,* Vol. II, 1983, Introduction.
3. C.A. Bayly, *Rulers, Townsmen and Bazaars: North Indian Society in the Age of British Expansion,* 1770-1870, OUP, Delhi, 1992, pp. 494-98.
4. Muzaffar Alam, *The Crisis of Empire in Mughal North India,* New Delhi, 1986.
5. N. Steensgaard, *Asian Trade Revolution of the Seventeenth Century,* Chicago and London, 1974.
6. Irfan Habib, "The Eighteenth Century in Indian Economic History", *Proceedings of Indian History Congress, (PIHC)* Calcutta, 1995, p. 358.
7. M. Athar Alit, "Recent Theories of Eighteenth Century India", *Indian Historical Review,* (ICHR) XIII (Nos. 1 & 2) pp.102-8.
8. Satish Chandra, *The eighteenth Century in India: Its Economy and the Role of the Marathas, the Jats, the Sikhs and the Afghans,* Centre for Studies in Social Sciences, Calcutta, 1991, p.17.
9. *Ibid.,* p. 16.
10. Ghulam Husain Tabatabai, who wrote *Siyaru'l Mutakhirin,* has drawn a convincing picture of large scale artisanal unemployment in Bengal. C.f. Irfan Habib's article "The Eighteenth Century in Indian Economic History", *PIHC.* Calcutta, 1995.
11. I have reached this calculation on the basis of details given in Francis Buchanan's, *An Account of Districts of Bihar and Patna in 1811-12,* Patna *(Hereafter mentioned as Buchanan).*
12. K.K. Datta, *Comprehensive History of Bihar,* Vol. III, Part I. Patna, 1976, p. 444.

13. Tapan Raychaudhuri, 'Non-Agrarian Production : Mughal India' in Tapan Raychaudhuri and Irfan Habib (ed.), *Cambridge Economic History of India.* Vol. I, p.278.
14. A.I. Chicherov, *India Economic Development in the 16th-18th Centuries : Outline History of Crafts and Trade,* Moscow, 1971, p, 231.
15. Buchanan, II. p. 639.
16. Those who made ornaments of glass (Kanch) were Muslims. *See Ibid*, p.620.
17. S. Chaudhuri, *Trade and Commercial Organisation in Bengal* (1650-1720), Calcutta, 1975, p. 151.
18. Buchanan, II, p. 640.
19. *Ibid.*, p. 666.
20. *Ibid.*, pp. 659-662.
21. *Ibid*, p. 266.
22. Sir H.H. Risley, *People of India,* 1908, pp. 76-77.
23. V.I. Pavlov, *Historical Premises for India's Transition to Capitalism,* Moscow, 1978, p. 212.
24. cf. *Ibid.*
25. Baines, *History of Cotton Manufacture in Great Britain,* p. 74. cf. S. Bhattacharya, *The East India Company and the Economy of Bengal,* London, 1954 , p. 183 .
26. Tapan Raychaudhury . "Non-Agrarian Production : Mughal India" in Tapan Raychaudhury & Irfan Habib (ed.). *CEHI,* p.291.
27. Francis Buchanan, .A *Journey from Madras through the Countries of Mysore, Canara and Malabar,* Vol. III. Madras 1807, p. 41.
28. Buchanan, II, p. 640.
29 P.J. Thomas, 'The Indian Cotton Industry' in *Modern Review,* February 1924, p. 136.
30. Buchanan, II. p. 646.
31. The word '*dadni*' derives from '*Dadan*' meaning advances.
32. Letter to Court. eighteenth January, 1754, in K.K. Datta (ed.). *Fort William-India House Correspondence.* Vol. I (1748-56), National Archives of India, Delhi. 1958. p. 762.
33. Irfan Habib, 'Potentialities of Capitalistic Development in the *Economy of Mughal India', Enquiry,* Vol. III, No.3, 1971. pp. 43-44.
34. Buchanan, II. p. 653.
35. A very similar type of manufacturing organization during the Mughal period was the *Karkhana* system. The Imperial *Karkhana* employed a wide variety of artisans - embroiderers, goldsmiths, painters, varnishers in lacquerwork, joiners turners, tailors. shoe-makers, armorers and the like - on a regular wage basis, but their primary object was to cater for the needs of the imperial court and the army, not production for the market. See Irfan Habib's 'Potentialities of Capitalistic Development in the Economy of Mughal India'. *op. cit.*, pp. 44-45.
36. See T. Raychaudhuri, "Some Patterns of Economic Organization and Activity in seventeenth Century India", cited in S. Arasaratnam "Weavers, Merchants and Company: The Handloom Industry in Southeastern India 1750-1790, *IESHR,* Vol. XVII. No.3. 1980 p. 259. Also see Irfan Habib, "Potentialities ..." *Enquiry*, Vol. III, No.3. 1971,. p.44.

37. S. Arasaratnam, ibid, p. 259. K.N. Chaudhuri too has referred to the distinction between the two methods. "The Structure of the Indian Textile Industry". *IESHR, Vol. XI.* No. 2-3, 1974, pp. 155-56.
38 Buchanan, II, pp.655-656.
39. *Ibid*, p. 653.
40. William Bolts, *Consideration on Indian Affairs,* London, 772, p. 191. cf. Debendra Bijoy Mitra, *The Cotton Weavers of Bengal (1757-1833),* Calcutta, 1978, p. 48.
41. Letter from Court. seventeenth March, 1767, in N.K. Sinha (ed.) *Fort William-India House Correspondence. Vol. V* (1767-69), National Archives of India. New Delhi. 1959, p. 303.
42. Debendra Bijoy Mitra, *The Cotton Weavers of Bengal (1757-1833),* Calcutta, 1978. p. 56.
43. See Appendix of D.B. Mitra, *The Cotton Weavers of Bengal* (1757-1833), Calcutta. 1978.

4

TRADE AND THE FOREIGN HAND

Patna was an important centre of inter-regional and international trade in Eastern India during the late medieval period. The city also emerged as one of the thriving centres of manufacturing, marketing, banking and entrepreneurial activities. It attracted the notice of foreign trvellers as a centre of cotton goods and silk stuff. Its commercial importance is also indicated from the name '*pattan*', meaning a mart[1]. Apart from cotton and silk goods, it had brisk inter-provincial trade in foodgrains and other commodities. The flowering of Patna for much of its urban-based economy and urban culture derived its strength largely because of its strategic location of being situated on the banks of the river Ganges and also partly because it had remained a political capital for a longer period of time. Both these conditions proved highly advantageous to its commerce and led to the proliferation of the trading and artisan classes of the city.[2] H.K.Naqvi is also of the opinion that the geographical setting of Patna paved the way for its commercial prominence. She has highlighted two important features in this regard. Firstly, the river Ganges being navigable throughout the year and secondly, its midway position between capital cities and rich doab on the west and plentiful Bengal possessing a convenient sea outlet in the east made it ideal centre of trade and commerce.[3] In fact, the location helped in shaping Patna as the main distributing centre for local goods as well as goods coming from different parts of the world. It emerged as a major transit depot between Bengal and upper India.[4]

Patna enjoyed the convenient river routes and land routes. It was flanked by the rivers on three sides which facilitated the movement of bulky and heavy goods through navigable rivers. The Ganges with its main tributaries and channels helped the merchants in reaching the most interior areas of Eastern India. Patna also remained in contact with Hugli and Dacca through the river route. Hugli was the principal port of the Dutch for the saltpetre trade and international trade. In the northern side, Patna was linked by the river route with Benaras. The same route connected Patna to the city of Agra and through the river Yamuna it was also linked to Delhi. The current of the river from Patna towards south-east was so strong that it could carry down frigates in five to six days, while the up-coming voyages took thrice the time.[5]

Patna, being a thriving trade emporium attracted merchants and travellers of European countries, who successfully tried their luck in the commercial transaction by forming Trading Companies at different points of time. Among them the Portuguese, the Dutch, and the English Trading Companies were mainly active in and around Patna.

The Portuguese were the first to enter Bihar[6]. They took full advantage of the cheapness of goods in Bengal and sold them at an enormous profit in their various ports all over India and beyond. For most of the sixteenth and seventeenth centuries, the raison d'etre of the casado[7] was trade, especially intra-Asia trade. Apart from Casado, Solterio[8] merchants, high officials and members of religious order also actively participated in the intra-Asia trade. S. Bhattacharya, feels that by the beginning of the seventeenth century the Portuguese power in the east began to decline mainly because of the disinterest and the withdrawal of the Portuguese state in the trading activities.[9] However, the real reason could have been the competition and threat posed by the Dutch East India Company.

The Dutch East India Company was founded in 1602 AD by a charter granted by the Dutch States-general and they sailed to the east with a determination to secure spices and other commodities for themselves. The company was named as 'De Verenidge Oost-Indische Compagnie' or 'the United East India Company. It was a chartered trading company closely attached to the Dutch state and its policies. The company was given the power and authority to wage war, conclude treaties, acquire territories and build fortresses. The Dutch first entered into Patna in 1632 and it is significant to note that their arrival here coincided with the expulsion of the Portuguese from Hugli by the Mughals in 1632 itself. The siege of Hugli by Shah Jahan affected the Portuguese trade at Patna as well and probably gave opportunity to the Dutch Company to establish trading relations. The Dutch established a factory at Patna and set up two saltpetre collection agencies in the neighbouring areas of Daulatganj and Singia. They were able to enhance their trade because of the exemption granted by the Mughal government.[10] By the beginning of the eighteenth century the Dutch had emerged as significant traders in and around Patna. Tavernier, a French traveller, who visited Patna on 21st Dec., 1665 writes "Patna is one of the largest towns in India..... The Dutch Company had an establishment there on account of trade in saltpetre which it refines on the right bank of (the) Ganges, 10 coss above Patna".[11] Ghulam Hossein Khan Tabatabi, the author of *Siyarul Mutakhirin*, wrote in the eighteenth century and he mentions that "the Hollanders ... had a factory at Azimabad, a house of great beauty and vast extent, nor was it quite destitute of strength being furnished with canon and men"[12]. However, the success of the Dutch was shortlived as the Dutch power had already began to decline in Europe by the end of the seventeenth century and the reflection of their weakness fell on their position in India as well. There was a gradual recession of their trading activities in the eighteenth century, but they still dominated the saltpetre trade at Patna. It was only during the second half of the eighteenth century that their monopoly was challenged by the English East India Company. The growing English trade posed the most intense competition and virtually outstripped the Dutch in Bengal trade after 1720 AD. The problem of the Dutch company were not confined to the competitions given by the English but the dishonest conduct of its employees also contributed to the growing financial and other problems.

The English also made Patna as their chief base of commercial operations in Bihar during the first quarter of the seventeenth century. In the beginning they were mainly interested in the trade of silk and saltpetre and two merchants named Robert Hughes and John Parker were appointed to look after the affairs. Their first factory at Patna was established in 1620, but soon shut down because of the loss. However, the trading activities of the English merchants continued in commodities like sugar and saltpetre. Again sometimes in 1650's a permanent factory of the English was established at Patna. During these years of the seventeenth century the English merchants could not withstand the monopoly of the Dutch merchants. It was only after the English East India Company got the diwani of Bengal in 1765, as a result of which they became politically and economically strong, that the Dutch monopoly at Patna was challenged.

Internal Trade

One of the important features of Patna's trading activities during the seventeenth and the eighteenth centuries was the inter-local trade. The inter-local trade was essentially a short distance version of inter-regional trade. In it markets such as periodic *hat*, *mandi*, *aurang*, *gunjes*, local *bazar* etc. played important role. The contemporary sources throw some light on the bazars of Patna. The areas around Patna like Singhiya, Chapra, Biharsharif, Lakhawar, Nandownepore, Salimpur, Baikatpur etc. offered wide range of commodities like cloth, indigo, slatpetre etc. The silk cloth was sent from Baikunthpur or Baikatpur to Patna, while cotton cloth was delivered from Lakhawar, Bihar sharif and other towns. The localities around Patna within a radius or nearly 50 miles, were important centres and markets of textile manufacturers, particularly *ambati* cloths and other fine and coarse varieties of calicoes. The commodities produced by artisans, were usually brought to these local marketing centres not only by artisans and peasants but also by traders who bought them directly from the producers. In 1620, English merchant, Hughes had purchased small parcel of '*ambati*' from the weavers of Luckhawar who had brought it to Patna town for sale in the local bazars. The calicoes which the weavers brought to the town bazar normally used to be raw or unbleached. Merchants used to buy these raw calicoes in huge amount and after bleaching they sent them to other markets. Silk cocoons, silk yarn of different varieties were also available at Patna. Patna, in fact, had to depend on adjacent Murshidabad and Saidabad and other parts of India for the unwound silk. This imported raw silk fulfilled the local demand of raw material at silk producing centres like Baikatpur which was known for Baikunthpur *alachah* and *tuckrees*, both intended for being used as women's petticoats. In addition to the local cotton goods, the city also collected goods from north Bihar. It included indigo, oil seeds, saltpetre, untanned leather, *ghee*, tobacco, rice, wheat, pulses, *makai*, wood, opium, sugar, *gur* fruits, 'Kokati' clothes, vegetables, fishes etc[13]. These products found their way not only to Patna but also to different parts of Bengal. There were exports from Patna to Mithila in good amount which mostly consisted of English clothes, indigo-seed, *bajra*, pulses, cotton, jute and spices. Mithila was connected by numerous rivers and, therefore, the trade in Mithila was mostly carried by river routes. The advent of European trading companies in the beginning of the seventeenth century had a tremendous effect on trade and commerce of Mithila-Patna. Several articles, sugarcane, tobacco, pepper etc. came to be produced on large scale from commercial point of view.

Patna also had commerical links with Tirhut, which was known for its saltpetre grounds. Prior to the advent of the Europeans in Bihar,

(Bihar) saltpetre was used for local purposes only like manure, cooling purpose etc. The dormant potentialities of Bihar as a source of supply of first class saltpetre were worked up only as a result of foreign reconnaissance, access and demand[14]. Patna was made the principal centre of supply of saltpetre and a collection centre, where saltpetre from the neighbouring areas like Singhia, Hajipur and Chapra etc. got stacked. Streynsham Master in his journey up the Ganges on 22nd September, 1676 AD, met 17 saltpetre carrying boats coming from Singhiya and Patna[15].

Patna also had brisk intra-local trade in food grains. As a chief rice producing area, Patna received a substantial quantity from adjoining areas like Tirhut, Monghyr, Purneah. Besides Patna, Sahabad and Tirhut were main exporter of sugar. Different varieties of pulses like *arhar, mung, khesari* used to be imported at Patna from Champaran, Biharsharif and Bhagalpur. Not only food grains, but dairy products too used to reach the local markets of Patna. Abul Fazl described the milk of Bihar *subah* to be 'rich in quality and cheap'. Tirhut and its adjoining areas were especially famous for its curd and *ghee*. Besides catering to the needs of local consumers, wholesalers and retailers Patna also acted as an emporia where dealers from other places secured their supplies. Infact, it was also a regional trading centre with extremely lively and well established trade links both by land and water with most regions of the country. In the inter-provincial trade, Patna had a peculiar importance as the meeting place for merchants who exchanged their cargo and money for western and eastern India. A wide variety of commodities ranging from goods for mass consumption to high priced luxury goods like silken goods, musk, furs, corals etc. were exchanged at Patna by the merchants and traders of different regions. The most important component of the inter-regional trade of Patna were the trade in food stuffs, textile products and saltpetre. Patna, which was known for its agricultural products, supplied food grains to various parts of India. It used to export wheat to Agra, Delhi and other parts on the western coast of India. It supplied food stuffs not only to the deficit areas on western coast but also to the rich province like Bengal. Patna as the main transit station between eastern and other parts of India also regulated the movement of foodstuffs that came from Bengal. According to Bernier, Bengal rice was carried up the Ganges to Patna[16] and from Patna it was sent to Agra, Masulipatnam and coast of Coromandel. Throughout the seventeenth and the eighteenth centuries there was much inter-provincial movement in rice. Besides rice, Patna also exported sugar, jaggery. During the period under review there was a 'great traffic'[17] in moist sugar at Patna. According to Ralph Fitch, the sugar of Patna was also carried to Bengal and other parts of India. A large quantities of food stuffs was also imported at Patna mainly from the region of Bengal. Not only sugar and rice but also commodities like salt, pepper, oil, mangoes, ginger, turmeric etc. came here. In Bengal, Hugly was the most important mart of salt and it had direct link with Patna. Pepper and other spices were usually imported at Bengal from Malabar coast of south-western India. Bengal thus acted as a link between the spice trade of Malabar coast and Patna. Some idea of the magnitude of trade in food stuffs and other commodities can be formed from account of Ralph Fitch and Manrique.[18]

Cotton goods were another major goods of consumption that entered inter-regional trade in pre-eighteenth century Patna. Virtually every part of the country had some varieties of textiles of export to other parts. While Gujarat and Bengal were known for its exquisite cloths, the cities like Patna, Deriabad, Chaireabad etc. were known for coarse variety of cloth known as *ambertee*. Compared to fine varieties of cloth, the trade in coarse and cheap cotton varieties was much larger as these were intended for use by the masses. Patna exported both fine and coarse varieties of calicoes to Bengal, Agra, Lahore and other parts of India. Throughout the seventeenth century there was a great traffic in products like *Ambati, Rasis, Zafarkhani, Jahangiris, Rahmoutes, Kaamsukha* etc. Patna also exported a type of coarse muslin known as *Cassa*[19], *Kaimkhani*. They were inferior in quality to muslin of Dacca, Malda, Santipur, and Sonargaon. It was chiefly bought by the Mughals[20], Praychees and Armenians in 1660s for transport to Lahore, north-west India and thence to Persia, Turkey and North Africa[21] .Besides muslin, the other products that were bought by them from the local market were *ambati* calicoes, *mandils* or turban cloths and *layches*. Patna was also known for its *chintz* but our sources are mute about its role in inter-regional trade. Whatever reference we get regarding the *chintz* is about international trade. Opium also figured in inter-regional trade of Patna and the main area to which it was sent was Malabar and mostly the Dutch merchants were involved in its trade. Besides Malabar, Patna opium was also sent to the local markets of Agra and Allahabad. About 34.5 per cent to 46 per cent was consumed in these markets[22]. Besides exports, Patna was also known for its imports. Being a major transit centre between eastern and northern India there was continuous flow of cotton goods. A large varieties of goods came at Patna from Orissa, parts of Bengal and upper India. From Orissa it received *malmali-Shahi*, *Sahan*, *Ginghams*, *Khasa*, and *Humum*. Besides Orissa, Bengal also supplied goods to Patna-*Sahan*, *Ginghams*, *rumals* from Hugli and Balasore; fine sashes and stripes (fine cotton cloth inter-woven with gold and silk thread) from Qasim bazar; *Dupattas* from Malda; *Khasa* and other variety of muslin from Dacca and adjoining areas. Thus, trade of *Hamams* and *Sahan* were in the hands of local Pathan dealers who imported them in small parcels from lower Bengal in boats. Before 1620-21 AD, these products were not in much demand for local consumption. The imports in these commodities increased because of the demands of the English factors. In 1620 AD, 60 pieces of *Sahans* and *hamams* were supplied by Patna factors to Agra factorys[23] . From upper India the products that came to Patna must have been *baftas*, and Jaunpur carpets. Though the major part of these goods was no doubt in transit, but it is possible that some quantity was being retained for local consumption.

Patna also had a flourishing silk products trade and a large quantity of silk products were imported – *Afghani*, *Charakhanas*, *Amari* from Orissa; silk and gold *orni*, *balaband*, *alejah* from Malda; *Tafetta* from Sherpur Murchai; *Satgaon quilts*, *Tassar* from bottom of Bengal and south-western regions. The import of these silk goods at Patna was regular, as it was not only carried for its own consumption but also for transmission westward such as Benaras, Allahabad, Delhi and Lahore. The Armenian traders were chiefly involved in the silk trade during the seventeenth century. As an enterpot Patna also received fine silk products of Gujarat for the Bengal markets. Apart from these finished goods, it also received unfinished goods for bleaching and other types of treatment. Specialisation in allied crafts such as bleaching, dyeing and printing by the weavers of Lakhawar led to considerable amount of traffic in unfinished goods such as *ambatis* and types of calicoes etc. Often unfinished products of Bengal were also brought for further treatment at Patna and other places. Printing on *Chinz* was only done at the factory of the Dutch at Patna. The calicoes which were woven in several places in Bengal were carried to Broach to be whitened with lemon water[24] . According to H.K. Naqvi, "the internal traffic in piece goods seems to have been concentrated mainly in the hands of native traders though there is evidence showing that the European traders also participated in it". Infact, compared to the European merchants, the native trader were more firmly established in the inter-regional trade as they enjoyed state privileges and also favour of local population who were not reluctant to interact with the foreign traders. Thus, throughout the seventeenth century the local merchants were left free from serious European competition in internal trade. Even during the eighteenth century internal trade largely remained in the hands of local traders and merchants, but in items like saltpetre, sugar and textile the Europeans began to monopolise the trade during this period of transition. Besides the trade in finished goods, there was a thriving trade in intermediate goods and raw materials, underlining a substantial amount of regional interdependence in important areas of manufacturing production[25]. The most important example of such inter-dependence was the trade between Bengal and Gujarat in raw silk and cotton. Large consignments of Bengal silk went to the cities of Gujarat like Surat, Ahmedabad and Agra *via* Patna. Pelsaert in his account has referred to Bengal silk being used in Gujarat. Merchants from Agra used to come to Patna for purchasing Bengal silk. On October 6, 1620 AD, the Patna factors sent a bale of silk containing grid, *katwai* and *shikasta* varieties for sale in Agra[26]. The raw material called *Serbandy* for local silk industry of Baikunthpur too came from Bengal, especially from Saidabad, Maqsoodabad and Qasimbazar. Trade in raw cotton also flourished at Patna and a large quantity of cotton from cotton tracts of Gujarat and Burhanpur came *via* Agra down the Ganges for Bengal.

Saltpetre was another item of internal trade, but it was highly dominated by the European companies, particularly the Dutch, who took great interest because saltpetre was the most coveted product in European market. Regarding its inter-regional movement the sources do not throw much light. Prior to European demand, saltpetre was used mainly for local purpose and the inter-regional trade in saltpetre was negligible. It was only after the advent of Europeans that the production and trade was revolutionized. The saltpetre of Patna used to be sent to Coromandel refining unit by the Dutch. Besides Coromandel, Patna saltpetre was also in constant demand at western and southern India. There was brisk movement in saltpetre, both raw and refined, under the Dutch and the English companies between Hugli, Balasore, Pipli, Kasimbazaar and Patna. In 1650 AD, the cost (of saltpetre) at Patna was only Re. 1 a maund and whereas at Hugli Rs 1-12 including customs and freight charges and at Balasore it was Rs. 2-10 a maund[27]. Regarding the local consumption, some ideas can be formed from the scattered data of the Dutch. Of the total refined saltpetre during 1680's 5.5 per cent was consumed within Bihar, while 11.75 per cent[28] was sent to different parts of Bengal. The rest was exported outside the region, probably to the European countries.

The internal trade centred around Patna also included variety of miscellaneous items such as gum, lac, musk, opium, perfumed pottery, shells or couries, etc. These items were largely exported from here. Some of the items like perfumed pottery, shells etc were obtainable only at Patna. The English East India Company always asked Surat agent to procure for them shells at Patna as these shells were used as small coins in India and in some parts of Africa. Even musk from the two feet high musk deer of the locality was available at Patna in very large quantity. The principal items of imports included corals, saffron, shawls from Kashmir, brocades from Benaras etc., most of which was locally consumed and a part of it also went to the smaller bazars in Bihar.

International Trade and the Foreign Hand

During the seventeenth and the eighteenth centuries the activities of Patna traders and merchants was mainly confined to the Indian territory.[29] The commerce of Patna began to spill out of the boundaries of India largely because of the efforts of Europeans. The Portuguese who had been active in the eastern part of India right from the middle of the sixteenth century, attempted to enter the market of Patna from its chief base at Hugli. The earliest reference of Portuguese trade at Patna have been found in the records of East India Company. The English factors observed in 1620 AD that, 'the Portuguese merchants... went to buy all they could lay hands on'. Every year their frigates came from Malacca and Cochin to their two ports Hugli and Pipli, where they had been licensed by the Mughal ruler Jahangir to live, and from there they came up to Patna with tin, spices, Chinawares and returned with commodities like *ambarti*, *cassa* silk, coarse Jaunpur carpets and all types of thin cloth dyed in red specially for the market in South. Besides, these commodities, the Portuguese had monopoly in salt trade throughout the province of Bengal . The articles that were imported to Patna, consisted of spices like cloves, pepper etc. from Malacca, Ceylon, Malabar; silks, semi-precious stones from China; sea shells or *cauris* from Maldives; bigger kind of shells called *chanquos* from Coromandel. A large number of expensive textile products like brocades, velvets, stains, escomillas (a fine cotton cloth like muslin) etc. were also brought by the Portuguese from Sumatra, Malacca, Borneo etc. The Portuguese were infact responsible for the movement of commodities between Patna and various south-east Asian countries.[30] Later on they preferred to trade with eastern Islands of Asia.

With the decline of the Portuguese trade and the appearance of the Dutch in Patna's economic activity there began a new chapter of high profit-yielding trade in commodities like textiles, opium, saltpetre, food stuffs etc. In Bengal which occupied a special position in production of high value textile like Dacca muslin, Patna had carved out an exclusive place in the output of coarse cotton cloth. Infact the trade of coarse cotton cloth was much larger in magnitude compared to exquisite textile products. The Dutch procured from Patna a large number of cotton textiles like *khasa*, *kamkhani*, Patna *Chintz* etc. for the markets of Japan, Ceylon, Indonesian archipelago, Holland etc. In 1701-2 AD the average price of *Khasa* was Rs. 8.50[31]. The corresponding price in company autumn sales in Holland in 1703 AD was Rs. 18.00[32]. By the early years of eighteenth century textiles were the biggest single item in the company's export bill from the region of Bengal. Fabrics accounted for about 43 per cent of the total value of the Dutch exports from India to Europe[33]. The Dutch, however, in seventeenth century were not interested in Patna's cotton and silk goods. The most important segment of the Dutch trade at Patna in seventeenth century was opium exclusively for the market of Indonesian archipelago. In 1740s the company's procurement was confined to Malwa variety but when the price of this variety began to go up at an alarming rate, it was replaced by Patna opium in 1648 AD. In 1642 AD, the cost of Malwa opium was Rs. 174 per 100 pounds where as in 1664 AD, the cost price of Patna Opium was reported to be Rs. 90 per 100 pounds[34]. The last quarter of the seventeenth century witnessed significant rise in the demand of Patna opium at Indonesia. The orders for 1673-74 AD and 1678-79AD, increased to more than 50,000 pounds[35]. In 1683 AD, the company had estimated the annual demand in the entire archipelago to be around 116,000 pounds[36]. Besides Indonesian archipelago, the Batavia council sold opium to Malay, Chinese and other merchants who carried it to Javanese ports of Grise, Japara, Cheribon; Palembang in Sumatra; Malacca in Malay Peninsula etc. In 1668 more than 55 per cent of the total output was sent to the international market. Prior to the Dutch, the Portuguese were also involved in the opium trade but the sources are silent on the magnitude of the trade. It appears that the Portuguese did not have flourishing opium trade like their successor, the Dutch. While opium was an item exclusive to the intra-Asian trade of the Dutch establishment, saltpetre figured exclusively in trade with Europe. For the Dutch the slatpetre had been of a great help during the wars with Spain and Hungary. Besides using it as an ingredient in the manufacture of gunpowder, the Dutch also used it as ballast for the homebound ships. The saltpetre trade began on regular basis in 1638AD during the reign of Subahdar Islam Khan. In 1658AD the company's procurement was about two million pound. In 1675 AD a number of leading salpetre merchants of Patna tried to constitute an oligopoly[37]aimed at producing exclusively for the Dutch. But since these merchants would have controlled the market, this offer was turned down by the company. In the initial stages the Dutch used to buy *kalmi* variety of saltpetre for the market of Holland but as the supply could not keep pace with the demand, it was replaced by *dobara* variety. It did so well that in 1669 AD the entire order was for this variety. Throughout the seventeenth century, Patna continued to supply salpetre and the average procurement of company in 1685-90 AD was 38,500 maunds.[38] Regarding the trade in food stuff at Patna the sources do not tell much. The only commodity that is referred is sugar, which was sent to Japan, Ceylon, Persia, Amsterdam etc.[39] Besides sugar, the company also exported rice, clarified butter, oil etc. from Bengal but in absence of source material it is difficult to figure out Patna's share in the export of these commodities. The overall value of goods the company exported from the region had increased from £150,000 in 1648-9 AD to £685,000 in 1652-3 AD. The volume of the Dutch import at Amesterdam was higher than that of England at London. The company not only participated in export but also import and the goods that were generally brought at Patna, consisted of spices, precious and non-precious metals etc. Among the spices that company imported were pepper, cloves, nutmegs, cinnamon etc. from Sumatra, Malay peninsula, Indonesian archipelago and Ceylon. The most important segment of import was procurement of precious metals from Asia and Europe. As is well known, the domestic production of gold and silver was negligible and the only other channel through which these metals were obtained was foreign trade.[40] During the seventeenth century, Kasimbazar, Hugli, Patna and Balasore were the principal bullion market of the east. Among the various types of silver that company sold in these markets, those from Japan usually tagged the highest price. In 1640-72 AD, import of silver from Japan figured prominently. Besides Japan, small quantities of silver bullion was also imported from Pegu, Arakan and Persia. The role of precious metals imported into the region was chiefly to provide purchasing power needed to buy the export goods. Not only silver but gold koban[41] and copper were also imported in the bullion market of Patna. It was obtained mainly from Japan. After 1680's, however, Japan ceased to be the chief source of precious metal for Bengal and the market came to be dominated by the Europeans, bar silver and silver coins,[42] which came from Red sea and Persian Gulf, where they found their way from Europe *via* the Levant. Most of the silver that were imported in Bengal were sold to *Sarrafs*, the professional dealers in money. But occasionally a part of it was sent to the royal mint also to be minted into *sicca* rupees as the Mughals followed a system of 'free' mintage under which imperial mints all over the empire minted coins at a small charge. In the context of import of precious metal by the Dutch at Patna, we see the transaction acquired a special significance as Patna[43] was one of the fine principal mints of the Mughals. The Patna mint[44] issued far more coins in gold, silver and copper than the mints of other regions. This was probably because of its position as a great river port where the Bengal and the upper Indian boats had their terminal so that silver was directly brought up to it from the Bay of Bengal.[45] Apart from Patna, the Bihar suba had another important mint at Rajmahal. Throughout the seventeenth century the Dutch and the other European powers used the Patna mint extensively. The Dutch company, apart from these principal commodities, also brought a substantial amount of miscellaneous items like nuts, sandalwood, sea shells, tin, lead, copper, sulphur, mercury etc. In the eastern region, for smaller payments, cowries formed a popular uncoined currency.[46] Besides sea shells, the copper coinage was also used in petty payments. Copper also served for vessels, and utensils, and for the ornaments of the poor.[47] The most important aspect of the Dutch trade at Patna was that the imports were almost entirely of Asian origin as the Dutch had extensive involvement in intra-Asian trade. This feature, infact, distinguished the Dutch from the other European companies. Their domination in the European trade depended substantially on their profit, in the intra-Asian trade. Another important aspect of the Dutch trade was the change brought in the nature of import. Prior to the coming of the Dutch, import was commodity based to a much greater extent. With the advent of the Dutch, the import of precious metal dramatically changed the commodity based import. Inspite of overwhelming flow of precious metals of foreign origin, the balance of trade remained in favour of the province. In the early years of eighteenth century approximately two-fifth of the total export to Europe was procured in Bengal.[48]

The English trading activity in the eastern part of India, started about the same time as the Dutch. In the initial year, they initiated the trade pattern of the Dutch. Their trading activity at Patna began with the arrival of Robert Hughes and Parker at Patna in June 1620 AD as has been mentioned earlier. On the arrival they found the Portugese already in possession of the market, but they just made their initial beginning. From July 1620 AD to June 1621 AD, the English invested a sum of Rs. 29,000, in addition to the money earned by the sale of their own goods.[49] The initial investment by the English factors was for the procurement of silk and cotton textiles. It is interesting to note that no mention of saltpetre was made by Hughes and Parker, among the products of Patna. The first orders for saltpetre was placed with the English company in 1624 AD by King Charles I, with a view to encourage them in its importation. The trading activity of English at Patna between 1600 and 1650 AD mainly consisted of textiles of various types. The establishments of a factory at Patna in 1620 AD was mainly for the purchase of local calicoes and Bengal silk. Different types of calicoes that were exported from Patna consisted of *ambatis, rasis* or *rasseyes*, *Zafar Khani*, *Jajahgeres*, *Sahan*, *Chautaha* etc. Another important variety of cloth exported from Patna was *Rahmoutes* or *Rawat* a kind of *Chautaha*. While the Dutch did not indent the varieties of *Choutaha* for Holland or Batavia, a fact which Pelsaert regretted, the English factors at Patna endeavoured to procure these for their investments.[50] Besides cotton textiles, the English also exported finished silk products and raw silk. Before the sixteenth century, the silk was imported to England from the markets of Persia, Syria, Berut etc. but because of the dearness of Persian silk, the English Factor in 1628-19 AD attempted to procure raw silk from Bengal. As silk cocoons, Skein (yarn) and cloth of different varieties were available at Patna at cheap rates the English factors decided to invest in it. Hughes invested Rs. 400 in *Tasar* goods that came to Patna from lower Bengal on trial, but the attempt did not succeed and it was left to Streynaaham Master to start the trade in the variable commodity. Besides *Tasar*, investment was made in Satgaon quilts, *Elachis* of Baicatpore, etc.

Apart from cotton and silk cloth, raw silk and raw cotton were also exported. Raw silk was imported in large quantities from Murshidabad and Saidabad in Bengal. The factors of the first commercial Mission to Patna set a bale of silk containing grid, *Katwai* and *.hikasta* varieties for sale in Agra. The textile procured by English in the first half of the seventeenth century were sent all over Europe and countries around Persian Gulf etc. A large number of miscellaneous commodities like sea shells, borax, gumlac, tin etc. were also exported from Patna. The English ships laden with Bengal goods often visited port of Basra, Persia, and England.

The trade scenario at Patna, however, changed, after the English East India Company was exempted for customs and transit duties by the *farman* of 1651 AD. They began to acquire a dominant position and this resulted in intense competition in procurement of various types of goods. An examination of Bengal factors annual explanation as to why the orders were not met in full from 1691 AD onwards, suggest that by far the most important reason why the Dutch were unable to procure the various varieties of textiles in the required quantity and the requisite quality was the tough competition by the English . Some idea about the commodities that were exported from Patna, in the second half of seventeenth century can be formed from the records of English factors. John Kenn, the chief at Cossimbazar from 1658-65 AD, in a note dated 1661 AD gave a list of commodities procurable at Patna (a) musk and drug of all sorts from Bhutan, (b) Turmerick, (c) Tinkall (Borax), (d) Gumlac, (e) *Taffetas*', *Ambertees, Sashes, Elachis*[51] . From the list of commodities, it is clear that textiles of Patna continued to be popular in the international market. The introduction of printed or stained calicoes called Patna *Chintz* in 1676 AD at England boosted the textile trade of Patna. In the course of only a decade the popularity of Indian textile goods had grown so much that in 1687 AD the Directors of the East India Company remarked that 'the Calicoes and Chintzes' had become the wear of ladies of the greatest quality. An attempt to check the rapid increase of Indian textile trade, was taken by passing an Act in 1700 AD prohibiting the importation into England, of all wrought silks, and stuffs mixed with silk, all calicoes painted dyed or printed or stained there. This Act had no effect on the import of Indian piece goods into English market for international consumption. The export continued to increase as the East India Company found a ready market in places like Amesterdam, Rotterdam in Europe. Infact, cotton goods of Patna remained one of the principal commodities on which commercial importance of Patna rested.

Saltpetre was another important commodity which brought Patna on the world map. The export of saltpetre from Patna in the second half to the seventeenth century was a new development in East India's maritime trade. Like the Dutch, the English demand for saltpetre was closely connected with national, political and military considerations. Salpetre obtained in Patna was at first sent home raw and this added considerably to the charges for freight and custom. The idea of sending raw salpetre was later abandoned and like the Dutch they too became particular about obtaining refined salpetre.

By the end of the eighteenth century the English had virtually monopolized the saltpetre production at Patna.

The English East India Company, emerged in the salpetre trade only at the end of the seventeenth century. In January, 1659 AD the English East India Company decided to send to Patna £5000 a year for its purchase as it could be bought at prices 40 per cent to 50 per cent cheaper than at Hugli. An idea about the cheapness of saltpetre can be made from the letter of James Bridgman. In December 1650 AD, he wrote that saltpetre was plentiful and cost at Patna was only Re.1 a maund and at Hugli Rs. 1-12 including customs and freight charges; and the saltpetre bought at Balasore cost about Rs. 2-10 a maund.[52] About 1665-70 AD the saltpetre at Patna was cheaper than on west coast, and at Masulipatanam. The annual requirement of the best saltpetre from Patna by the English alone was 800 to 1000 tons[53] (1671 AD). The whole amount of saltpetre collected at Patna was sent to Hugli and other ports to be exported to European countries. The saltpetre trade of the English continued to flourish in the eighteenth century amidst the competition for procuring saltpetre by different Eurpean and non European traders. In an attempt to oust the Dutch, the English in 1732 AD ordered no less than 70,000 maunds of saltpetre.

Regarding the opium trade of English in the seventeenth century the primary sources do not provide enough information. There were a few local dealers of opium in Patna, who amassed huge fortunes by sale to foreign merchants. The English trade in opium reached unprecedented heights in last quarter of the eighteenth century and beginning of the nineteenth century when they smuggled opium into the Chinese territory.[54] The opium bought at Chinese ports of Canton and Macau consisted mainly of Patna opium, which was cheaper than the Malwa opium.

The English were not only involved in export but also in imports of various commodities at Patna. In the beginning of seventeenth century the English imported several articles like broad cloth, quick silver, vermillion, lead, tin, amber beads, coral, swords, knives, five wares etc. Amber beads corals were brought by English to Patna from Agra and Surat. The Revenue Records of English Company mention additional commodities of Pepper, Peepal (red chillies), coconut, brimstone, quick silver and Chinaware.[55] Among imports, as mentioned earlier, bullion had the highest demand in India since the imports from India were valued in England and Indian merchants were naturally paid in bullion. The volume of Bengal trade in outward direction can be judged from the fact that in four years from 1680 to 1683 taken together, the English, imported into Bengal silver worth £ 200,000 to pay for their purchases. In August 1677 AD four chests of bullion were sent along with some broad cloth and lead to enable the Patna factors to clear off their debts accounting to Rs. 23,000 and to procure investments.[56] Copper was also in demand at Patna. Here it was used partly for coinage and partly for dispatch to Benaras and Gorakhpur. The price of copper varied from Rs. 45 to Rs. 50 per maund. Among other articles of import, tin and lead brought from Malaya and Sumatra occupied an important place. Lead was sold in the market for Rs. 6 to Rs. 8[57] per maund where as tin for Rs. 38 per maund[58]. Apart from bullion, the most important article of import were woollen clothing of different types coming under the one genetic name of broad cloth. There was not much demand for this commodity among the masses but it was prized by the aristocratic classes more particularly those in upper India. Large quantities of broad cloth used to be sent to Patna, for further dispatch to Delhi and neighbouring areas. However, the trade of broad cloth at Patna did not prove to be profitable. In the second quarter of the eighteenth century, Patna council decided to send back to Calcutta all the ordinary broad cloth, since there was no prospect of selling it there. Another commodity which was brought by the English in the first half of seventeenth century was an imported article called bone-lace, a kind of linen. One significant feature of the seventeenth century trade was that there was little demand for British goods at Patna, and therefore, the balance of trade remained in favour of Patna. An important point to be mentioned here is that while the English brought bullions from home, the Dutch obtained a good part of precious metals within Asia through an active participation in Intra-Asian trade.[59] Towards the end of seventeenth century, Patna, because of its commodities of the international acclaim, became one of the most important trading stations in Asia for all European trading companies, specially the Dutch.

Dadni System was the chief mode of business activities of the European merchants. In this system, long before the advent of season for a particular commodity, the merchants used to reach the actual cultivator or manufacturer through the local small agents or *Paikars* and advanced money to them so as to obtain right for the purchase of a particular commodity. During the period under review, the European trading company's procurement organization at Patna also followed this system. The precise proportion of the cash advance to the value of the contract was obviously a matter for negotiation, but the norm appears to have been between 50 per cent to 65 per cent. Sometimes, a part of the advance was given in goods imported by the company. For example, the English East India Company advanced broad cloth as *dadni*.[60] Not only advance payment was given, but often the merchant were provided with company's *dastaks*, enabling them to transport goods to be supplied to the company, without any transit duties. Robert Hughes, in the early seventeenth century, reported a diverse system of advance by North Indian merchants to weavers at Lakhawar. These merchants invested principal money either in form of ready cash or bills of exchange. Another important aspect of mode of procurement at Patna was that there were different specialized brokers in different varieties of goods. In the seventeenth century Bihar, advances were not only made in weaving but also in many other trades like saltpetre, opium etc. The wealthy contractors (*asami*) employed agents, who advanced money to the saltpetre producers *(nunia)* and received the saltpetre from them and delivered it to the East India Company.[61] In this system of *dadni* the most important role was played by the extremely heterogenous group of middlemen, who generally used to be salaried employees. They were the most important link between the company and the merchants, who worked on the basis of commission or brokerage from the buyer and seller. Usually the brokerage used to be 0.5 per cent of the price of the goods from the buyer and 1 per cent from the seller[62]. However, on basis of correspondence of Patna factors it could be assumed that the brokerage was uncertain and fluctuating. The Dutch company, which used the services of an opium exporter in the seventeenth century, paid Re 1 per case of 145 pounds examined.[63] According to Manrique, in 1629-43 AD there were about 600 brokers and middlemen mostly wealthy at Patna. It appears that these brokers were the well-off section of the society. However, an English merchant describing the small middlemen catering for the trade in 1620s said that "they are so poor and beggarly that they cannot furnish us without entrusting them with money before hand"[64]. The overwhelming dependence on this system of advance at times created problems for the trading community. Often the goods accepted by trading company from a particular merchant used to be less than the sum of money advanced to him. Besides, many artisans, weavers in particular, normally used to sell the finished good to the third party. Infact, the company and the *dadni* merchants were always involved in disputes about balance and about the quality of product. In cloth trade, absence of standard units of measurement increased the difficulties and usually the weavers suffered loss. Another significant feature of the *dadni* system was that a large amount of money which used to be given as advance was often tied for long period. For example, advances for cotton piece goods might began upto nine or ten months before the cloth would be received.[65]

Patna also had a fairly advanced system of banking and credit in the hands of merchants and professional money changers called *sarraf*. The banking houses played a key role in the trade and money lending during the medieval period. Hiranand Shah, a Marwari from Rajputana, arrived in the city in the reign of Shah Jahan and founded the great banking houses of Jagat Seth. Later on his eldest son Manikchand, the *Nagar Seth,* established a banking house at Dacca. Besides banking, there were various commercial practices but the most important practice was issuing of *Hundi* or bill of exchange.[66] The English factors in India usually remitted money from one factory to another through instrumentality of *Hundi*. The English Factors in the early seventeenth century at Patna, depended for funds for the investment on the remittances of the Surat and Agra factors through bills of exchange. The first supply of money in bills of exchange of Rs 5000 came by February/March, 1621 and by August, the total amount received was Rs. 32,000 besides Rs. 4,000 constituting the sale proceeds.[67] The bills of exchange were issued by the Agra factors in the name of well known *Sarraf* at Patna, the most important being Chand Sahai Sao.[68] Besides Chand Sahai Sao, the bill of exchange from Agra also used to be send in names of Sunder Maya Das, Man Mukund or Makhann and Bisheswar Das. At times, the Patna factors had to face difficulty in encashing the Agra bills of exchange. For example, in March 1621 AD, one bill to the value of Rs. 1500 was at first rejected as it was not written by Shahu. The changes for remitting money varied between various places and it was by no means fixed.

Infact, the charges fluctuated. Thus, when in 1621 AD, the *Sarrafs* of Patna were suddenly called upon to transfer Rs. 300,000 to Agra there was sudden fall in the exchange charge on payments from Agra to Patna. Not only English factor, but the administrator of Patna also used *Hundi*. Muqarrab Khan, the governor of Bihar, on being transferred from the province in 1621 AD delivered Rs. 3 lakhs to the *Sarrafs* of Patna. Tavernier opines that the exchange goes up to Patna to be repaid to him at Agra. Regarding the rates of discount at Patna, Tavernier opines that 'the exchange goes up at Patna from 7 per cent to 8 per cent. The usual rate was 1 and ½ per cent. The *Sarrafs* must have had substantial income owing to the activity in transactions and by the discount allowed in the exchange. According to Irfan Habib, in the seventeenth century the *Hundi* was made to serve both ends (i.e. remittance of money and short term credit), but the difference was that while in first case it was drawn by *Sarraf*, in the second the drawee was most often a merchant. The local moneylenders and merchants were not only involved in monetary transaction but also in large scale buying up of goods. For example, in 1620 AD, the Chief banker of Patna in a deal with Robert Hughes, an English merchant, gave an assurance that next year he would provide brown *ambartis* as desired.[69] Thus, before the eighteenth century, there was a flourishing financial transaction on large scale.

Portuguese

Therefore, we observe that the commercial organization of the Portuguese, the Dutch and the English trading companies in India and at Patna particularly rested on a common structured form throughout the seventeenth and the eighteenth centuries. Their basic feature was a head settlement or factory situated at or near some major Indian port with subordinate stations in the interior where many of the export goods were produced. These settlements were normally independent of one another, though close operational ties were maintained between them. Normally all the European trading companies initiated the methods adopted by each other in order to pursue their imperialist and colonial designs. For example, both the Dutch and the English took over from the Portuguese the practice of demanding pass money from the Indian merchants in return for guaranteeing protection from their own ships. They also sometimes followed the typical European practice of naval blockade. In important trading areas where Europeans lived and traded under the jurisdiction of the Mughal officers, the threat of a maritime blockade, preventing the indigenous ships from leaving the ports, was the European answer to their vulnerability on land[70]. However, so long as the Mughal rule remained strong the European companies were very careful to keep even the local authorities in good humor and desisted from taking any overt action which was likely to create misunderstanding. But with the decline of the Mughal authority during the first half of the eighteenth century and the resultant internal disorder emboldened the European companies to firmly establish themselves in different regions. This led to rivalry and there was a fight for supremacy among these companies in different regions at different points of time. But in relation to the country power they were broadly guided by some sort of professional brotherhood and a symbiosis, and they tried to put up a joint front against the local Indian resistance. This we have already discussed in chapter 1.

By the end of the eighteenth century, the English East India Company was able to monopolise the production of various goods at Patna. The artisans who were involved in the production of goods, used at the local level were not much affected since the European trading companies, especially the English hardly took interest in monopolizing such production. But artisan based industries like textile, saltpetre and sugar were drastically hit by the monopolistic control by the East India Company. The figures of export available for the late eighteenth century and the early nineteenth century do not show any decline in export of these items in terms of rupees and also in quantity. Rather, there is a tremendous increase in the export of such goods. However, this is for sure that this increase in export was at the cost of the production done by the artisans at a smaller level.

Therefore, the figure provided by Francis Buchanan of the total exports as seen in the following table is highly misleading.

Table 4.1 : Items of Export and Imports from Patna District

	Articles of Commerce	*Export (in rupees)*	*Imports (in rupees)*
1.	Shukkar	54,000	26,300
2.	Cotton cloth	5,45,000	38,500
3.	Banusa Cloth (Tasar and Cotton mixed)	1,24,000	6000
4.	Cotton-Woollen and Shutranji	22,000	2000
5.	Chintz	1,23,500	15,400
6.	Blankets	7,800	2,820
7.	Goldand Silver thread lac	15,000	650
8.	Saltpetre	12,600	—

Source : Francis Buchanan : *An Account of the Districts of Bihar and Patna in* 1811-12. Table No. 44, pp. 776-78.

Buchanan at one place during his description has mentioned that "the Saltpetre was exported to Calcutta, now entirely on the company's account..."[71] In other words, the local artisans like *nuniyas* had totally lost their hold in saltpetre production by the end of the eighteenth century. Precisely because of company's monopolistic control and the resultant decline of artisans, we get reference to the emergence of a broker class called *Delals* in large numbers in the beginning of the nineteenth century. "There are a good many *Delals* or brokers, who have no capital engaged in trade, and live by making bargains for others. In Patna, they have the shopkeepers under a good deal of subjection, and scarcely any purchase, even to the value of one rupee, can be made without their interference, and of course they enhance the price by the amount of their commission."[72] There is no denying the fact that the traders and merchants prospered even during the second half of the eighteenth century, but they were largely involved in the regional trade and that too in items of local consumption. The export and import of more profitable items like saltpetre and cotton textile remained in the foreign hands.

NOTES

1. The mart is generally defined as a place of trade and probably there is an implied sense of seaport trading centre of the peninsular seaports with '*Pattana*' ending.
2. For an alternative argument on the emergence of towns and cities see Gavin R.G.Hambly, 'Towns and Cities: Mughal India', in Tapan Raychoudhuri and Irfan Habib (eds.), *The Cambridge Economic History of India,* vol.I, Orient Longman, Delhi, 1982, p.438. Herein the author argues that centres of commerce and manufacturing possessed a *raison d'etre* far transcending short-lived political upheavals and revolutions, just because most Indian urban centres depended for their prosperity upon political conditions favourable to the steady pursuit of their particular trades and specialized craft industries. He feels that trade and commerce could be disastrously affected by a climate of political instability, especially if that instability threatened to become prolonged or to spread itself over an extensive area.
3. Hameeda Khatoon Naqvi, *Urban Centres and Industries in Upper India (1556-1803),* Calcutta, 1968, pp.97-98.
4. Sukumar Bhattacharya, *The East India Company and the Economy of Bengal,* London, 1954, p.127.
5. Cited in H.K.Naqvi, *op. cit.*, p.98.
6. Infact, the Portuguese were also the first to enter into India via the sea-route.
7. The literal meaning of Casado was a married settler and infact it was used as judicial category to denote a permanent resident of a settlement of the Eastado da India. See Sanjay Subrahmanyam, *The Portuguese Empire in Asia 1500-1700*, Longman, London and New York, 1993, p.231.

8. Solterio was a free wheeling merchant without a permanent residence in any Portuguese settlement.
9. For a detailed analysis on the decline of the Portuguese trading company's in the East see Sukumar Bhattacharya, *The East India Company and the Economy of Bengal,* pp.69-70. A more forceful account in this regard based on various Portuguese sources has been given by Sanjay Subrahmanyam, *op-cit*. The Attitude of the Mughal Emperor Shahjahan towards the Portuguese is also significant in this regard especially when we take up the case of Hugli and its sieze by the emperor. The sieze of Hugli was disastrous for the Portuguese trade in the East. The defeat of Mughal army against Adil Khan of Bijapur was used as a plank to strike the blow at the Portuguese because Shahjahan attributed Adil Khan's success to the help which he got from the Portuguese.
10. The imperial *farman* issued in November 1642 AD was the first document to exempt the company from the payment of transit duty on the Pipli-Agra route which passed through Bengal, Bihar and part of North India. In accordance with this *farman* five *nishans* were granted by Shah Shuja, the Provincial Governor, to the Dutch which exempted the company's goods from transit and other duties on Pipli-Patna route.
11. Jean Baptiste Travenier, *Travels in India*, Vol. I, V. Ball (tr.), London, 1889, pp. 121-2.
12. Qeyamuddin Ahmad, 'Patna-Azimabad (1540-1765) A Sketch', in Qeyamuddin Ahmad (ed.) *Patna through the Ages, Glimpses of History, Society and Economy,* Janaki Prakashan, Patna, 1988, p.75.
13. Upendra Thakur, *Aspects of Society and Economy of Medieval Mithila*, Janaki Prakashan, Patna, p. 112.
14. Jagdish Narayan Sarrkar, *Glimpses of Medieval Bihar Economy 13th to mid eighteenth century,* p. 71.
15. Jagdish Naryan Sarkar, 'The Saltpetre Industry of India in the seventeenth century with Special Reference to Bihar' *Journal of Bihar and Orissa Research Society* (hereafter JBORS), 1937, p. 337.
16. Francois Bernier, *Travels in the Mughal Empire AD 1656-1668,* A Constable (tr.& ed.) p.437.
17. Travernier, *Travels in India*, Vol. II, (tr. & ed.) by V. Ball, p.23.
18. Manrique remarked that 'so extensive is the trade that over one hundred vessels are yearly loaded up in the ports of Bengal with only rice, sugar, fats, oils, wax and similar other articles'.
19. '*Cassa*' or '*Khassa*' was a local product of Patna but in the list of imports particularly from Orissa and Dacca there is also reference of it. It appears that it was not only produced locally but a small quantity of it was also imported probably from Dacca and Orissa.
20. The term 'Mughals' during the period under review, was used to refer all sorts of Central Asian merchants including Persians and merchants from North West frontier.
21. Jagdish Narayan Sarkar, 'The cotton trade of Patna in early seventeenth century', *The Indian Historical Quarterly*, Vol. XII, March 1936, No. 4, pp. 645-657.
22. Om Prakash, *The Dutch East India Company and the Economy of Bengal 1639-1720*, p. 58.

23. Jagdish Narayan Sarkar, *Glimpses of Medieval Bihar Economy 13th to mid eighteenth century*, p. 74.
24. Om Prakash, *op. cit.* p. 149.
25. Om Prakash, 'Some Aspects of Trade in Mughal India, *Proceedings* of *Indian History Congress,* 1981, p. 175.
26. Jagdish Narayan Sarkar, 'The silk trade of Patna in early seventeenth century, *The Indian Historical Quarterly,* Vol. 15, 1939, p. 224.
27. Jagdish Narayan Sarkar, *Glimpses of Medieval Bihar Economy. 13th to mid eighteenth century,* p. 73.
28. Om Prakash, *The Dutch East India Company and Economy of Bengal 1630-1720*, pp. 59-60.
29. Here by Indian territory we mean present day India i.e. independent India.
30. See Sanjay Subrahmaṇyam, *op. cit.,* pp. 230-35.
31. Om Prakash, *op. cit*., pp. 61-62.
32. *Ibid.*
33. Chicherov, *India, Economic Development in the sixteenth eighteenth century, Outline History of Crafts and Trade,* p. 115.
34. Om Prakash, *op. cit*, pp. 147-48.
35. *Ibid*., pp. 149-152.
36. *Ibid*., p. 153.
37. Oligopoly was some kind of an association of merchants.
38. Om Prakash, *op. cit.,* pp. 59-60.
39. *Ibid*., p. 173; HK Naqvi, *op. cit*, p. 253.
40. Om Prakash, 'Some Aspects of Tarde in Mughal India', *PIHC*, 1981, p. 173.
41. Koban was an oval shaped Japanese coin, containing 85.69 per cent gold, 14.25 per cent silver and 06% alloy.
42. The silver coins that were imported consisted of coins such as Mexican, Seville, Spanish rials, rials of eight, six, provincial corwn, lion, cross dollars, dukatons. From Persia also came coins like venetian and Sequins. see Om Prakash, *The Dutch East India Company and the Economy of Bengal*, p. 54; Manucci, Vol. II, *op. cit*, pp. 393.
43. Apart from Patna, the other mints were at Lohore, Ahmedabad, Jaunpur, Tanda (which was later shifted to Rajmahal). Hassan Nishat Ansari in his article'Numismatics in Bihar' has discussed in detail about the mints of Bihar. According to him, Patna mint was established during the reign of Firoz Shah Tughlaq by Prince Fateh Khan, the heir- apparent but it opened for a very brief period. On the basis of Shahukhi coin of emperor Babur, on which the mint name has been read as patnah or Patna, he has concluded that it was one of six Indian mints of Babur.
44. Abul Fazal, *Ain-i-Akabari*, Vol, I, by Blochman (tr.), p. 32.
45. Aziza Hasan, 'Mints of the Mughal empire', *Proceedings of Indian History Congress,* Part I, Patna 1968, p. 325.
46. Jadunath Sarkar, *History of Bengal (Muslim Period 1200-1757)*, p. 217.
47. Irfan Habib, 'Monetary system and prices', Tapan Raychaudhuri and Irfan Habib (eds.), *The Cambridge Economic History of India*, vol. 1, p. 37; HK Naqvi, *op. cit*., pp. 246-7.
48. Om Prakash, *The Dutch East India Company and the Economy of Bengal,* p. 53.
49. HK Naqvi, *op. cit*., p. 101.

50. Jagdish Naryan Sarkar, *'The Cotton Trade of Patna in Early seventeenth century'*, *IHQ*, Vol XII, March 1936, Nov. 4, p. 645. Infact, the cotton industry at Patna in the early half of the seventeenth century was regarded as better suited to English East India Company's demand than that at Samana in Patiala district.
51. N.N. Ray, *The Annals of the English Settlement in Bihar*, Kamal Book Depot, Calcutta, 1927, p. 51.
52. Jagdish Naryan Sarkar, 'The Saltpetre Industry of India in seventeenth century with special reference to Bihar, *Journal of Bihar and Orissa Research Society*, 1937, p. 349.
53. Jagdish Naryan Sarkar, *Glimpses of Medieval Bihar Economy*, p. 71.
54. The English East India Company were able to procure opium from the cultivators of Bengal after they got *diwani* of Bengal in 1765, and then they smuggled these opium to Canton. The bullion that they got out of the sell of opium was used for purchase of tea in China, which was then exported to England. The kind of trade is referred to as the 'Triangular Trade'.
55. HK Naqvi, *op. cit.*, p. 113.
56. Jagdish Narayan Sarkar, *Glimpses of Medieval Bihar Economy*, p. 105.
57. Jagdish Narayan Sarkar, *op. cit.*, p. 82.
58. Jagdish Naryan Sarkar, *Ibid*, p. 82.
59. Om Prakash, 'Some aspects of trade in Mughal India', *Proceedings of Indian History Congress,* p. 184.
60. S. Bhattacharya, *op. cit*, p. 130.
61. Chicherov, *op. cit.*, p. 162.
62. *Ibid.*, p. 162.
63. Om Prakash, *The Dutch East India Company and the Economy of Bengal*, p. 106.
64. Chicherov, *op. cit.*, p. 121; Jagdish Naryan Sarkar, 'The Silk Trade of Patna in Early seventeenth century, *IHQ*, Vol. 15, 1939, p. 227.
65. P.J. Marshall, East *Indian Fortunes*, p. 36.
66. *Hundi* was a promised payment after a specified period at a particular place and allowing a discount which included interest, insurance changes and cost of transmission of money. In long distance trade, this form of payment fulfilled the requirements of an expanding demand for credit and it also reduced the risks involved in the transmission of cash to distant places.
67. Cited in Jagdish Narayan Sarkar, *Glimpses of Medieval Bihar Economy,* p.107.
68. Ibid.
69. Chicherov, *op. cit.*, p.162.
70. K.N. Choudhary, 'European Trade with India', in Tapan Ray Chaudhuri and Irfan Habib (eds.) *op. cit*, pp. 391-392.
71. Francis Buchanan, *op. cit*, p. 680.
72. *Ibid.*, pp. 697-698.

5

EUROPEAN FACTORS

Impact on Crafts and Artisans

By the end of eighteenth century, the British East India Company had been successful in fulfilling its need for export of different products such as saltpetre, cotton, sugar etc. As a deliberate colonial policy, the English used their power to alter the conditions of production and the existing relationships between the artisans and themselves.[1] The system of advance payment to the weavers by the East India Company had yielded the desired result and contributed to increasing the textile procurement and trade of the English Company at the turn of the century.[2] But at the same time came the exploitation of indigeneous artisans and the gradual ruin of the local crafts. The colonial policy of monopolising the trade and raw material did not give a clear sign of the motive the company held. The exploiting tendencies could be visible only after the oppression of artisans started in real terms with various regulations e.g. on weavers (See Appendix III). However, a closer examination would reveal that the detrimental effect of colonial policy began as early as 1765. According to Bolts, the trend of expansion of industry in India was checked after 1765 by the establishment of the English monopoly over the trade and production of various goods at Patna. The growth of the industries was arrested and they began to decline.[3]

As mentioned, the oppression of artisans, specially weavers, had already started by the end of eighteenth century. In the meantime, came the disastrous famine of 1770. Due to scarcity of foodgrain about fifty people died of starvation everyday in the streets of Patna in January 1770.[4] In 1773, a statement was submitted of the number of families in eleven villages of *pargana* Muner and fiften villages of *pargana* Arrah in the district of Patna. In 1769, the number of families in those twenty-six villages were 556 but in 1773 the number was 282.[5] This indicates the extent of depopulation in these areas. The whole population was affected by this famine and so were the artisans and craftsmen. A large number of skilled weavers, spinners and cotton growers died.[6] The total output of cotton goods declined at most of the cotton weaving centres.[7]

Another contributing factor for the deteriorating condition of the craftsmen was the underpayment by the company. The weavers who received the company's advances did not get a fair price for their labour. They were obliged to work against their will at whatever prices were arbitrarily imposed on them. The Company's own men admitted that their European rivals were prepared to pay 20 per cent to 30 per cent more and naturally the weavers were unwilling to work for the Company .[8] Even Buchanan indirectly attacks the mode of payment to the weavers -"Each man on becoming bound (*Asami*) to the Company received two rupees, and engaged not to work for any person untill he had made as the Company required... The agent orders each man to make a certain number of pieces of such or such goods, and he is paid for each on its delivery, according to the price... This shows clearly that the system of advances is totally unnecessary, but it is here pursued by all the native dealers, as keeping the workmen in a state of dependence little better, if so good, as slavery."[9] It is important to note here that even during and after the famine of 1770 when yarns had become 25 per cent dearer than before, the price paid by the Company remained the same.[10] E.E. Pote, Resident of Patna stated in 1791 that the weavers did not like to enter engagements with the Company on the Company's rates. He examined the prices of the raw material and labour to ascertain if the rates given to the weavers were really low. He found that in reality the rates given to the weavers were very low.[11] Even in the beginning of the nineteenth century the same situation prevailed. The profit of the cotton was not enough to buy all items of daily necessities. In the table 5.1, the profit on coarse and fine cloth in few divisions of Patna district are given.

With such a low profit one could hardly expect the weavers to flourish. In fact, Buchanan admits "that in these districts the weavers were bound to act as porters for conveying the goods of travellers."[12] About the carpet-weavers'profit, it is mentioned that "each small carpet required one ser thread worth 10½ annas, and dying 1½ anna; the value is 18 annas, two men make one piece in two days, and each has only 1½ anna a day profit ."[13] The use of word 'only' is significant in the above quotation from Buchanan and it reflects that 1½ anna was not enough for the subsistence.

Table 5.1 : Estimate of Profit of Weavers in Patna District

Division	*No. of weavers*	*No. of looms*	*Type*	*Total profit in a month for each loom.* *Rs.*	*Annas*
Patna City	1810	1892	Gajji (Coarse)	2	12
Gaya	2120	2500	Solegaji (Coarse)	1	9
Behar	5400	6000	Tangjeb (Coarse)	1	14
Daudnagar	2175	2500	Charkhana (Coarse)	2	6
Jehanabad	Not Available		Amriti (Fine)	2	2

Source : Francis Buchanan, *An Account of Districts of Bihar and Patna in 1811-12*, passim.

The British official accounts too acknowledged the cause of weavers' dissatisfaction in Patna. Their unwillingness to accept company's advancces was due to the little profit. By weaving coarser cloths for the private traders, for which there was a general demand, they secured higher profit.[14] E.E. Pote, the Resident in Patna informed that the weavers told him openly they would not receive the Company's advances. Their reply was "markets are open and they will sell their cloths where they please. Let the Company go to the markets or establish Cooties and if they choose they will bring their cloth to Cooties for sale and if they do not, they will carry from elsewhere but they will not enter into engagements whatever with the Company. (I begged them that I will settle the price before them so that they might judge how fairly the Company meant to deal with them.) They declared 'no'."[15]

Interestingly, despite so much reflection of resistence, the weavers worked for the Company. Why? May be the weavers looked upon the Company with unlimited power and so could not easily defy their authority. At the same time, the artisans had no alternative but to work for the company. The trade of the other European companies and private merchants had gradually declined by the end of the eighteenth century and the Company's employment was the only alternative left to them. A change of occupation might not have been an easy process particularly in view of their hereditary skill. Now, atleast they were assured of some income for survival of their family. But this direct employment by the Company reduced the flexibility which the aritsans had previously possessed and it was the Company which was now the sole beneficiary.[16]

Similarly, the condition of salt manufacturers was in a flux. Buchanan himself has informed that the East India Company paid a low price to the native manufacturers. To add to the pressure, the company agents paid even lesser than what company offered for the natives. "The contractors or *pykars* were paid by the company at the rate of Rs. 1.14 as for one maund of saltpetre supplied, but they paid Rs. 1-6 annas only to the *nuniya*".[17] The zamindaras also exacted 6 or 7 rupees a year illegaly from each furnace.[18] The *nuniya* also "had to give one-half of their produce to the government as *Sayer* for the manufacture of saltpetre, out of which one-fourth was paid to the zamindars on whose estate the *Kooties* (furnaces) were situated as *Malkana* . ... *Besides* paying revenue to the government and *Malkana* to the proprietors of the soil, the *nuniya* had to pay *salami* and *russoom* to the *Moostajeers* and others which amounted to about Rs. 6.8 as per year on each *Kooties*."[19]

The impact of colonization on artisans and craftsmen went hand in hand with the decline of various crafts. In Patna, the demand for fine cloth had diminished, but coarse cloth continued to be produced by the majority of the weavers.[20] The picture that Buchanan drew was of a well developed cotton textile industry, but the superior varieties were already feeling the impact of a reduction in orders from the Company. By the mid nineteenth century, the situation had changed completely which is evident from the statement of the Commissioner of Patna Division - "It appears that twenty years ago a brisk trade was carried on in the manufacture of cloth at Jehanabad, and Behar, which has in the former place entirely ceased, while in the latter the amount of manufacture is very limited, in consequence of the cheap and durable goods from Manchester with which the native manufacturers are unable to compete."[21] Though Buchanan's table presents a glittering picture of numerous flourishing production centres of *gajji* (a type) "but by the end of the nineteenth century this was all that was left of a great industry in Patna and Behar... of questionable antiquity."[22] Similarly, the silk industry had also declined.[23] Blanket-weaving and carpet weaving industry too was on decline. The monograph on carpet weaving says - "Twenty years ago when the handloom industry of Patna was in its last stage, one Lain Mian of Patna who was a maker of cotton cloth and *Satranjis*, conceived the idea of utilizing the ordinary handloom in the manufacture of *darris*. Since then, this handloom manufacture called *Karga darris,* has made vast strides."[24]

Saltpetre industry at the local level also suffered a decline with the establishment of East India Company's factories in Patna district. Though the demand for saltpetre within Patna district among the natives was "...very considerable both for gunpowder and fireworks",[25] but the company forcibly asked the local manufacturers to supply crude saltpetre. They were given advances on the condition that they would not sell or provide saltpetre for any other (the Dutch or the French) than the company.[26] Most of the saltlpetre world market was captured by the East India Company. Interestingly, the company's investment in saltpetre was more during times of peace than in the war time.[27] During thirteen years of peace from 1764 to 1776 the total quantity of the saltpetre sale was 295,673 bags, during the six years of war from 1777 to 1782 the sale declined to 76,059 bags. Again during ten years of peace from 1783 to 1792 the quantity of saltpetre sale increased to 331,301 bags.[28] This shows that the British monopolised the saltpetre trade so as to fulfil their war ends and requirements.

There were, however, few industries like leather, woodwork, pottery and metal which continued to flourish,[29] as their market was mostly confined to the adjoining regions of Patna district.

What were the reasons for the decline of major crafts well-established in Patna district?[30] The withering touch of the Company's tariff policy, the one-way free trade, importation of machine-made goods brought about the ruin of the handicrafts[31] and other local industries. The export of mill-produced English goods proved disastrous to the cotton textile industry. Due to unmatched competition between mill manufacture and hand-made goods in the foreign markets, Indian fabrics began to lose market which led to further decline in the output. This feature is, at all events, quite perceptible at Patna, so that we may conclude that there the industry had reached a stage where stagnation had set in due to East India Company's monopolizing trends.[32] The English exports of manufacturers not only practically wiped out the Indian exports of cotton goods but also entered India to challenge Indian manufacturers in their home market. Crawfurd has estimated that British cotton goods import in India in 1837 accounted for only 6 per cent of the total value of India's domestic textile production.[33] But Irfan Habib believes that in as much as the competition of British manufacturers had also wiped out Indian textile exports of a value over 2 million pounds, the total fall in the value of Indian production should have been about 11.5 per cent.[34]

The one person who is dead against any view supporting any sort of decline of handicrafts ever since 1963 is Morris D. Morris.[35] He is not in favour of accepting the role played by British made goods in bringing about the collapse of handicrafts in Patna district and whole Bengal during the first quarter of the nineteenth century. This stand of Morris has evoked criticisms from different scholars and it is still relevant due to the variety of reasons.

Morris did not believe that cotton weaving was a highly developed crafts before 1800, which does not hold true atleast for Patna district. We have already seen the flourishing condition of various industries. He disagreed with the notion that Manchester machine-made textiles wiped out the Indian handicrafts by the mid-nineteenth century. His logic is that Manchester exported both yarn and cloth. While British cloth was competetive with Indian handloom production, machine-made yarn seems to have strengthened the competitive position of the indigeneous handloom sector despite the fall in prices.[36] He argues that the demand for cloth in India seems to have been fairly elastic, and the fall in price led to a movement down the demand curve. Again, there seems to have been a shift to the right of the demand curve for cotton cloths. He further said that not only was there population growth, there was also changes in custom which increased the amount of cloth per capita. Morris pointed out that there was a shift away from inferior to cotton fabrics. He concludes - "There is evidence of rising demand for cotton cloths during the nineteenth century. The vast expansion of British cloth exports to India skimmed off the expanding demand. The handloom weavers were atleast no fewer in number and no worse off economically at the end of the period than at the beginning."[37]

This view has been questioned on various accounts. The first one to investigate the fact was Daniel Thorner.[38] He thoroughly described what cannot be called industrial growth and what is industrial decline. He defined the concept of "deindustrialisation" as a decline in the proportion of the working population engaged in secondary industry to total working population, or a decline in the proportion of the population dependent on secondary industry to total population. In Patna district, the East India Company discontinued its cloth investment after 1819 and the factories located there were closed.[39] This resulted in the unemployment of thousands of weavers engaged in factories and all of them flocked into agriculture sector. Salt manufacturers also faced the same fate with company's monopoly over salt.

Morris gives evidence of a steady rise in the per capita income to prove his point of growth of industry. But what he seems to have missed here is the simultaneous increase in prices of essential food items like rice. We are not in access of any data showing the increase in price of rice in Patna district during the beginning of the nineteenth century, but we do have evidence of such increase in adjoining regions. For example, at Benaras the price of rice per mound in 1792-93 was only Rs. 6-10-8, which almost doubled by 1822-23 and was as high as Rs. 12-8-0 per maund.[40] The increase in prices of essential items was bound to affect the real income of artisans.

Toru Matsui[41] also questions Morris and his argument that the machine-made yarns strengthened the competitive position of the indigenous handloom weavers vis-a-vis British weavers. Matsui questioned if from these premises, one can safely draw the conclusion that the handloom weavers were no fewer in numbers and no worse off economically at the end of the period than at the beginning or that the net effect for the economy was a positive one in terms of per capita real income. Matsui further pointed out that even if we accept that a sharp fall in the price of yarn helped the handloom industry, it gave a bitter blow to the indigenous spinning industry. Matsui argued that the demand for cloth increased because the price fell, not that the price rose because the demand increased. What happened was that there was a sharp fall in prices. We have then reasons to infer that Patna handloom weavers tended to be worse off, which even Buchanan in his account has acknowledged.[42] The fall in the prices of yarn was caused by the innovation in the spinning process in Britain, while the decline in the prices of cloth as caused by the innovation in the weaving as well as spinning process. Matsui concludes that "it follows that from the long range point of view the fall in price of cloth per piece was greater than the fall in price of yarn required for one piece of cloth. It is clear then that the renumeration for weaving per piece was less. "[43] According to Buchanan, each man on becoming bound to the company received two rupees, and engaged not to work for any person until he had made as the company required.[44] This affected the weavers adversely. The way to cover the decrease in renumeration was to work harder and for more and more hours but there was a physical limit to hard work. We have grounds for supposing that the Indian handlook weavers became worse-off economically or fewer in number during this period.[45]

Irfan Habib has also questioned the stand of Morris that changes in fashion increased the cloth consumption. He argues that while it was true that low prices of imported manufactures increased the total quantity of the cloth consumed, "the further implied assertion that the total value of cloth consumed in India also increased substantialy, at any rate by a higher percentage than that of the value of imported cloth to previous total consumption, is quite baseless."[46] The statistical table given by Buchanan also shows that consumption of finer cloth may not have been substantial in Patna district and that is why there is comparatively fewer production of such cloths.[47]

Amiya Kumar Bagchi[48] is more specific in his arguments and does a micro study of gangetic Bihar to examine whether there was a case of deindustrialization. To prove his point he compares the figures compiled by Buchanan for Patna district with the 1901 Census estimates relating to the same district. Bagchi proceeds with the definition of deindustrialization given by Daniel Thorner and shows that there was a decline in the proportion of working population of artisans to the total working population between 1809 and 1901. He concludes that "the process of deindustrialization proved to be a process of pure immiserisation for the several million persons whose material condtions had been surveyed by Buchanan between 1809 and 1813."[49]

We may, therefore, conclude that the East India Company was solely responsible for the declining condition of crafts and craftsmen in Patna district. It was a part of the colonial policy of exploiting the resources of a colony by England. England had just gone through a century of revolution and the industries needed raw material for enhanced production capacity. It began with the purchase of Indian cotton and other raw materials. The company also needed items like saltpetre to wage a revolutionary war in Europe. Along with it arose the demand for a huge market and they had India as ready-made market. And with this process of taking away the raw materials and sending in the finished products the death of local artisans and craftsmen began. It was only those artisans who produced items like shoes, woodworks and goods for local consumption, survived. The worst affected were the skilled workers connected with cotton, silk, carpet, blanket and saltpetre.

NOTES

1. S. Arasaratnam, "Weavers, Merchants and Company", *IESHR*, XVII, No.3, 1980, p.257.
2. K.P. Mishra, 'Textile Manufacture and the Company's Trade in late eighteenth century North India', *PIHC* (48th Session), Goa, 1988, p. 458.
3. W. Bolts, *Considerations on Indian Affairs,* London, 1772 Chapter XIV, passim.
4. Cited in Nikhil Sur's article "The Bihar famine of 1770", *The Indian Economic and Social History Review,* XIII, No. 4, 1976, p. 526.
5. N.K.Sinha, *The Economic History of Bengal, II,* 1970, pp.51-52.
6. D.B. Mitra, *The Cotton Weavers of Bengal (1757-1833),* Calcutta, 1978, p. 53.
7. *Ibid*, p. 53.
8. *Ibid*, p. 62.
9. Francis Buchanan, *An Account of Districts of Bihar and Patna in 1811-12,* Vol. II, Patna, p. 653.
10. Cited in D.B. Mitra, *op. cit.*, p. 64.
11. *Ibid*, p. 109.
12. Buchanan II, p. 654.
13. *Ibid*, p. 657.
14. *Proceedings of Board of Trade,* 22nd January, 1788, Proceeding No. 8, Vol. 64, cited in D.B. Mitra, *op. cit.*, p. 35.
15. *Ibid*, 4th September, 1787, No. 84, Vol. 60, cited in .B. Mitra, *op. cit.*, p., 135.
16. K.N. Chaudhuri, "The Structure of Indian Textile Industry in the Seventeenth and Eighteenth Centuries", *Indian Economic and Social History Review,* Vol. XI, No.,2-3, 1974, pp.160.
17. cf. K. K. Datta (ed.), *CHB, Vol. III,* Part I, Patna, 1976, p. 451.
18. Buchanan, II, p. 667.
19. cf. K.K. Datta (ed.), *op. cit.*, p. 452.
20. Buchanan, II, p. 652.
21. *India, Revenue Proceedings,* June 1864, p. 343, Reply 419 of the Commissioner, Patna Division, 25 February, 1864.
22. N.N. Banerjei, *Monograph on the Cotton Fabrics of Bengal,* Calcutta, 1898, pp. 26-30.
23. W.W. Hunter, *A Statistical Account of Bengal, XIV,* Delhi, 1976, pp. 180-81.
24. N.G. Mukherji, *Monograph on Carpet Weaving in Bengal,* Calcutta, 1907, p. 248.
25. Buchanan, II, p. 664.
26. *Letter from J. Wintle, Magistrate of Bhagalpur to T. Brown, Commercial Resident of Patna, dated seventeenth October 1803.*
27. *Journal of Indian History,* April 1941, Supplement, p. 814.
28. *Selection from unpublished Correspondence of the Judgea-Magistrate and the Judge of Patna,* edited by K.K. Datta, pp. 28-29.
29. J. Krishnamurthy, "Deindustrialization in Gangetic Bihar during the nineteenth century: Another look at the evidence," *IESHR, XXII,* No.4, 1985, p. 415.

30 Barring a few, there is almost a unanimity among the historians who assert that there was a decline in nineteenth century. See Morris D. Morris, "Towards a Re-interpretation of Nineteenth Century Indian Economic History", *IESHR,* V, No. 1, 1968.
31. Sunil Kumar Sen, "Economic Transition in Bengal". *The Asiatic Society Seminar Series - I, "Renascent Bengal"* (1817-1857), Calcutta, 1972, p. 21. Also see Syed Badrul Hasan, *Yadgar-e-Rozgar,* Patna City, 1931, pp.72-74.
32. H.K. Naqvi, *op. cit.*, p. 144.
33. K.N. Chaudhuri (ed.), *Economic Development of India under the East India Company,* Cambridge, 1971, pp.239-42.
34. Irfan Habib, "Colonization of the Indian Economy (1757-1900)", *Essays in Indian History,* Delhi, 1995, p. 320. See also his "Studying Colonialism without Perceiving it."
35. Morris D. Morris, "Towards a Re-interpretation of the Nineteenth.Century Indian Economic History", *Journal of Economic History, Vol. XXIII,* No.4, December, 1963, pp.606-18.
36. *Ibid*, p. 611.
37. *Ibid*,. p. 613.
38. "Deindustrialization in India, 1881-1931", in Daniel and Alice Thorner, *Land and Labour in India,* Bombay, 1965, pp. 70-81.
39. K.K. Datta (ed.), *CHB, Vol.III,* Part I, p. 448.
40. D.B. Mitra, *op. cit.*, p. 125.
41. Toru Matsui, "Towards a Re-interpretation of the nineteenth Century Indian Economic History", *IESHR,* Vol.V, No.I, 1968.
42. Buchanan. II.
43. Toru Matsui, *op. cit.*, p. 21.
44. Buchanan, II, p. 653.
45. *Ibid*, p . 21.
46. Irfan Habib, "Colonization of Indian Economy", *Essays in Indian History,* Delhi, 1995.
47. Buchanan, II, Table Nos. 42 and 43, pp. 774-75.
48. Amiya Kumar Bagchi, "Deindustrialization in Gangetic Bihar, 1809-1901," *Essays in Honour of Prof. S. C. Sarkar,* New Delhi, 1976.
49. *Ibid*, p. 519.

6

SUMMARY AND CONCLUSIONS

The geographical divisions of the various *pargana* falling within the boundary of Patna district in 1811-12 remained more or less same as they existed during the earlier times. Only three new *pargana* were added later. These were Baikunthpur, Shahjahanpur and Dinapur. There are some changes in names of these *pargana* also. Since the majority of the *pargana* remained unchanged from the Mughal period to the eighteenth and nineteenth centuries, some degree of administrative continuity is reflected. However, after the coming of the British East India Company the political and economic situation changed and this affected Patna district also. The British changed the physical shape of Patna according to their requirements. All the administrative measures were the result of the emerging situation and a deliberate move to consolidate the position of the British in the region.

As Patna happened to be an important trading centre of Eastern India in the eighteenth century (and even earlier), the European companies established their factories in large number here. There was constant rivalry among these European companies and ultimately the East India Company emerged successful. It also managed to get a monopolistic control over the production in Patna district by the end of the eighteenth century.

Textile, saltpetre and sugar industries were the main industries of Patna district. These were the items in which British were more interested and so gradually they began to monopolise their production. Though the artisans who were involved in items of local consumption were not much affected, those involved in textile, saltpetre and sugar industries, were hard hit by the monopolistic control by the East India Company. The figures provided by Buchanan of the total exports of different items shows that the production was in flourishing condition once.

But as we have seen that after 1819 all the textile factories in Patna were closed and the production of saltpetre no more remained

Table 6.1 : Tems of Exports and Imports from Patna district (1811-12)

Article of Commerce	*Exports (In Rupees)*	*Imports (In Rupees)*
1. Shukkar	54,000	26,300
2. Cotton cloth	5,45,000	38,500
3. Banusa cloth (Tasar & cotton mixed)	1,24,000	600
4. Cotton woollen and Shutranji	22,000	2,000
5. Chintz	1,23,500	15,400
6. Blankets	7,800	2,850
7. Gold and silver thread lace	15,000	650
8. Saltpetre	12,600	

Source : Francis Buchanan: *An Account of the Districts of Bihar and Patna in 1811-12,* Table No. 44, pp. 776-78.

in the hands of local *nuniyas,* the artisans would have suffered to a great extent. The weavers could not withstand the competition from the mill-made British clothings. Similarly, with the establishment of many sugar factories in Patna by the British, the local manufacturers were badly affected.

It is difficult to form an exact idea of the affected population of the artisans in Patna district but it could be safely concluded that the size of population engaged in weaving, spinning and other branches allied to it, salt manufacturing and sugar manufacturing was considerable and they all faced the wrath of colonisation.

For those artisans, whose profession or specialisation was a whole-time occupation, may have been left with no alternative but poverty and starvation. But a notable thing is that the cessation of export markets for Indian handmade products with the coming of the low-priced British goods did not mean extinction of the cotton weaving, spinning, salt manufacturing or sugar manufacturing altogether as a profession. There was a considerable demand of these items within Patna district itself. The profession of those weavers who were engaged in the manufacture of the finest quality of cloths was no doubt gone for good, but there were certain other fabrics which were best and cheaply manufactured by hand e.g. carpets, shawls, embroideries etc.However, the supply of these items was confined to the local market.

The wage figure and the profit of different artisan types available to us show that they may not have been left with enough money to live comfortably.

Table 6.2 : Profit of Different Artisan Types in Patna District (1811-12)

Type	*Profit (per month)*	*Remarks*
1. Torch maker	3 Rupees	
2. Pagribund	3 to 5 Rupees	
3. Lac ornament maker	4 to 6 Rupees	
4. Glass worker	2 Rupees	
5. Distiller	13 Rupees	A very comfortable subsistence[1]
6. Kasera	7¼ Rupees	
7. Brick layer	3 to 4 Rupees	Principal artists received double[2]
8. Dhuniya	3 to 4 Rupees	Often paid in grains[3]
9. Spinner	3¼ Rupees	
10. Cotton weavers	3 to 4 Rupees	
11. Kangnigar	$3\frac{7}{16}$ Rupees	
12. Chintz maker	5 to 6 Rupees	
13. Carpet weaver	3 to 4 Rupees	
14. Blanket weaver	15 ½ Rupees (a year)	
15. Sugar manufacturer	1¼ anna	
16. Salt manufacturer	7 rupees (a year)	The manufacturers could not live by such a pitance[4]

Source : Francis Buchanan, *An Account of the Districts of Bihar and Patna in 1811-12*, passim.

We observe that most of the artisans made a profit of Rupees 3 to 5 a month which was not sufficient for them to live an easy life as has been recorded by Buchanan. Only distillers are said to have made a profit of Rupees 13 a month, but then they were supposed to pay a heavy duty to the government sometimes as high as Rs. 7 a day.[5]

Thus, we do not get an overall rosy picture of the artisans of Patna district. Their condition was bad during late eighteenth and early nineteenth centuries which became worse after the decline of major industries as a result of monopolistic control of production and other regressive measures by the British.

NOTES

1. Buchanan, II, p. 631.
2. *Ibid*, p. 646.
3. *Ibid*, p. 647.
4. *Ibid*, p. 667.
5. *Ibid*, p. 631.

Appendix I

CLIVE'S LETTER TO COURT OF DIRECTORS, CALCUTTA, 30th SEPTEMBER, 1765

I have at least, however, the happiness to see the completion of an event, which in this respect, as well as in many others, must be productive of advantages hitherto unknown, and at the same time prevent abuses that have hitherto no remedy. I mean the dewanee (Diwani) which is the superintendency of all the lands and the collection of all the revenues of the provinces of Bengal, Bihar and Orissa. The allowance for the support of the Nabob's dignity and power, and the tribute to his majesty, must be regularly paid, the remainder belongs to the company. Revolutions are no longer to be apprehended; the means of effecting them, will in future be wanting to ambitious Musselman, nor will yours servants - civil or military-be tempted to ferment disturbances, from whence can arrive no benefit to themselves. Restitution, donation money etc; will be perfectly abolished as the revenues from where they used to issue will be possessed by ourselves. The power of supervising the provinces though lodged in us, should not however, in my opinion, be accepted. Three times the present number of civil servants would be insufficient for the purpose; whereas if we leave the management to the old officers of government, the company need not be at the response of one additional servant, and though we may suffer in the collection yet we shall always be able to detect and punish any great offenders, and shall have some satisfaction in knowing that the corruption is not among ourselves. By this means also the abuses inevitably springing from the exercise of territorial authority, will be effectually obliviated; there will still be a Nabob with an allowance suitable to his dignity and the territorial jurisdiction will still be in the chiefs of the country acting under him and the presidency in conjunction, though the revenues will belong to the company. Besides were the company's officers to be collectors, foreign nations would immediately take umbrage and complaints preferred to the British court might be attended with very embarrassing consequences. Nor can it be supposed that either the French, Dutch or Danes will acknowledge the English company - Nabab of Bengal, and pay into the hands of their servants the duties upon trade, or the quit rents of those districts which they have for many years possessed by virtue of the royal phirmound or by grants from former Nabobs. Your revenue, by means of this new acquisition, will, as near as of can judge, not fall short for the ensuring year of 250 lakhs of sicca rupees, including your former possessions of Burdwan etc; hereafter they will at least amount to 20 or 30 lakhs more. Year civiled military expenses, in time of peace, can never exceed 60 lakhs of rupees. The Nabab's allowances are already reduced to 42 lakhs of rupees, and the tribute to the king is fixed at 26. So that there will be remaining a clear gain to the company of 122 lakh of six rupees or pound 1,650,900 sterling, which will defray all the expenses of the investment, furnish the whole of the China treasure, answer the demands of all your other settlements in India, and leave a considerable balance in your treasury besides. In time of war, .when the country may be subject to the incursions of bodies of cavalry, we shall notwithstanding be able to collect a sufficient sum for our civil and military exigencies and likewise for our investments, because a very part of the Bengal and Bihar dominions, are situated to the .eastward of the Ganges, where we can never be invaded. What I have given you is a real, not imaginary state of your revenues and you may be assured they will not fall short of my computation.

Appendix II

LIST OF ARTISANS IN PATNA DISTRICT

S. No.	Class of Artisans	Type I Who produced for upper class II Who produced essential items III Who produced for common man	Total number in Patna Distt.
1.	Laheri (Lac ornament maker)	I	343
2.	Shishaghur(Glass blowers)	I	3
3.	Bleachers/Washermen	I & III	2582
4.	Thathera	III	402
5.	Kasera (Vessel repairer of copper, brass & bell metal)	I	478
6	Khandiyar (Worked in horn and ivory	I	4
7.	Pinjrasaz (Iron cage maker)	III	5
8.	Sonar (Goldsmith)	III	2293
9.	Jelahgur (Gold and silver polisher)	III	3
10.	Tubukgur (Maker of gold and silver leaf)	I	14
11.	Achfurosh (Dyers of cotton thread with Morinda)	III	3
*12.	Weaver of Tsar silk	I	2246 (782 houses)
*13.	Weaver of cotton cloth	II	79600 (19900 houses)
14.	Kangnigar (Put gold and silver thread in fine cloth)	I	50

(Contd.)

1	*2*	*3*	*4*
15.	Butabanwaiya (Women who flower cloth)	I	95
16.	Chhapagar (Printed gold and silver flowering)	I	17
17.	Cintz maker	I	269
18.	Carpet weaver	I	209
19.	Tashbaf (Weaver of cloth of gold and silver)	I	3
20.	Gotasaz (Weaver of gold and silver lace)	I	50
21.	Batwaiya or Kalabatu (Maker of gold & silver lace)	I	50
22.	Alukbund (Made ornamental knots for daggers)	I	6
23.	Nakad (Twisted silver thread)	I	10
24.	Paper maker	III	64
25.	Umbrella maker	I	5
26.	Tailor	II	900
27.	Puzayah (Brick workers)	II	1182
28.	Thatchers	III	1027
29.	Barhai (Carpenter)	II	3128
30.	Lohar (Blacksmith)	II	1219
31.	Lohar & Barhai (Both)	II	513
32.	Sungturash (Stone-Cutter)	II	84
33.	Kumhar (Potter)	II	2900
34.	Dhunia (Cotton Cleaner)	II	1873
35.	Spinner of cotton	II	330396
36.	Dyer or Rungrej	II	552
37.	Nilgur (Dyers with indigo)	II	5
38.	Kundikor (Who betle bleached cloth)	II	24
39.	Patwar (Knitter of string)	II	345
40.	Soap makers	III	77
41.	Candle makers	I	12
42.	Oil makers	II	20531 (5132 houses + 3)

(Contd.)

1	*2*	*3*	*4*
43.	Bari (Torch and Platter maker)	I	162
44.	Dustarband or Pagriband (Turban makers)	I	12
45.	Tent maker	I	12
46.	Abirgar (Red starch maker)	III	12
47.	Churisaz (Bangle maker)	III	282
48.	Tikisaz (Glass ornament maker)	III	126
49.	Garland maker (Mali)	III	813
50.	Ink-maker	I	6
51.	Petara maker (Basket maker)	III	13
52.	Morasaz (Stool maker)	I	7
53.	Mohurradar	III	13
54.	Guddi-maker (Kite-maker)	III	57
55.	Atushbaz (Fireworks)	III	118
56.	Book-binder	I	15
57.	Kalaigur	III	25
58.	Kanghaigur (Haircomb maker)	III	8
59.	Nalbund (Horse-shoer)	I	15
60	Leather workers	Both I & III	3561
61.	Khadimbund (Maker of frames of looking glasses)	I	2
62.	Rangdhaluya (Tin ornament maker)	III	101
63.	Panni (Tin leaf maker)	III	44
64.	Nitre maker (saltpetre)	III	2264 (566 furnaces)
65.	Wire makers	I	96
66.	Butter makers (Makkhaniyas)	III	13
67.	Sweet makers (Halwai)	III	1708
68.	Potters who make toys	III	49
69.	Gulalsaz	III	12
70.	Parchakush or Andiya (who smooth fine cloth with needle)	I	31

(Contd.)

1	*2*	*3*	*4*
71.	Kharadi (Turners who make wooden wares)	III	37
72.	Newargar (Weave cotton tape)	III	13
73.	Knitter of mitten	III	2
74.	Blanket Weaver	III	564
75.	Kangjar (Rope Maker)	III	7
76.	Redlead maker	I	22
77.	Singriph maker	I	1
78.	Naychahbund (Hooka maker)	I	97
79.	Nariyali hooka maker	III	44
80.	Diyawal (Cotton wick maker for lamps)	III	3
81.	Preparer of Tobacco	III	253
82.	Charcoal ball makers	III	114
83.	Majun makers (a kind of intoxicating sweetmeats)	I	7
84.	Distillers of rose water and essence	I	8
85.	Sangur cutlers	I	1
86.	Sikulgur or armourers,	I	109
87.	Tirgur (Arrow makers)	I	3
88.	Needle makers	III	2
89.	Bidri makers	I	1
90.	Minamurussa (Gave ornamental colours, made false stones for rings)	I	3
91.	Mohurkund or seal engravers	I	1
92.	Pajaya	I	14
93.	Mulumbasaz or gildar	I	2
94.	Sugar boilers	III	36
95.	Indigo manufacturers	III	7 (No. of factories)
		Total	464500

Source: Francis Buchanan, *An Account of Districts of Bihar and Patna in 1811-12;* Table No. 41.

**Note:* Here we assume that in each house atleast four members worked on loom and furnace on average. Buchanan has written that each loom required one man and women, but at the same time he has said that the whole family was involved in weaving and in manufacturing of saltpetre. Further, though Buchanan has fixed a ratio of six to a house, one cannot assume that all the six were capable of contributing the production one way or the other. That is why, a ratio of four artisans to a house has been put.

Appendix III

REGULATIONS FOR THE WEAVERS

The Regulation for weavers of April 1782 were aimed against interlopers. It was recorded in the *Proceedings of Board of Trade (Commercial)*, 3rd June, 1783 Prog No.30, Vol. 37.

It provided "that the purchasers of the said cloths apparently knowing them to be the property of the Company by the secret and clandestine manner which they take to procure them or by the notoriety of the weavers being in the Company's employ who offers to dispose of them, on proof of the fact, shall be liable to punishment by the adalat, according to the nature of their offence and cloths so purchased shall be confiscated".

On 18th July, 1786, 21 regulations were passed. Some of the regulations were as follows:

Regulation No. IX provided "And for the better ascertaining the number of weavers in each district in the Company's employ as well as the nature and extent of their respective engagements, it is hereby directed that every weaver be furnished with a ticket specifying the name, the place of abode and cooty under which he works and containing an account of the dates and periods of advances made, the value of the cloths of goods he shall from time to time deliver in return."

Regulation No.X provided "that at the end of each year or expiration of each management, the Commercial Resident or his representative shall sign to the adjustment of such weavers' accounts and receive the wearers' signature to the counterpart thereof, which latter shall remain at the Factory or Cootey to be produced whenever called for".

Regulation No. XI : "Upon any weaver failing to deliver, cloths according to the stated periods agreed upon, the Company's agent shall be at liberty to place peons upon them and keep them under restraint."

Regulation No. XII: "If any weaver in the Company's service

should be convicted of selling cloth either by himself, any of his family, journeymen or by any agent to any other merchants or dealers whatever whilst he is deficient in his deliveries according to the stated periods of his agreement with the Company, such offender shall be punished in a regular process and conviction in the judicial Courts".

Regulation No. XIII: "And whereas a practice has prevailed of selling cloths provided by the Company's advances clandestinely to the individuals apparently because it suits private dealers best to buy without risking balances, ready-made goods and those of the finer assortments which the Company's weavers long supported by them and enabled by their advances, produce."

"It is hereby resolved and ordered that the purchasers of the said cloths apparently knowing them to be property of the Company by the secret and clandestine manner which they take to procure them or by the notoriety of the weavers being in the Company's employ who offer to dispose of them, on proof of the fact, shall be liable to punishments by the Adaluats according to the nature of his offence and the cloths so purchased shall be confiscated".

Regulation No.XIV: "And whereas it has been alleged by those whose interest it was to make such purchases that the Company's weavers cannot be distinguished from others, it is hereby ordered that a list or register of the weavers employed by the Company in every Pergunnah be stuck up by the Company Agent those in the Cutcherry of that Pergunnah and the same to be corrected at the beginning of every week or month according to the alteration that shall have happened in the week or month preceding."

Regulation No. XVII: "Weavers with whom compulsion is used to enter into agreements or who are not paid for their cloths according to the agreements voluntarily made between them and the Company's servants or contractors, may complain in the first place, if injury is offered by native agents, to the Commercial Resident, or contractor under whom they act; if the injury is offered by the Resident or Contractor himself, or if he gives no redress against his agents, complaints may be made to the Collector of the district in which such weavers reside and the said Collector is hereby required to enter into an intelligent and impartial examination of such complaint and if he judges it expedient to represent the same to the Commercial Resident or Contractor, to receive his answer and determine thereupon either to dismiss the Complaint or to refer it to the Presidency and the weavers if dissatisfied with the conduct of the Collector may themselves represent their case at the Presidency. But in order that the encouragement may not hence be taken for false or frivolous complaints, in the view of eluding the performance of fair argument or of procuring improper advantages, all manufacturers are hereby informed that Complaints which are found to be really groundless will be duly punished, and of this, Collectors are also desired to take proper notice".

Another set of Regulations was issued on the 23rd July, 1787.

Regulation I : "The weavers shall give at least a fortnight's notice when they intend not to take further advances".

Regulation II: If they have not fulfilled their engagements by the period agreed on, they shall not work for newer engagements nor for bazar sales, until those engagements are completed."

Regulation III: "When any weaver fails to deliver cloths, at the stipulated period he has engaged for, the Company's agent or representative shall be at liberty to place peons upon him, in order to quicken his deliveries"

Regulation IV : "If notwithstanding, any weaver shall by himself or any other persons, sell cloths to private merchants, European or natives, dealers or agents of whatever kind, whilst he is deficient in his stipulated deliveries to the Company, such offender may be prosecuted in the Dewanee Adalat and upon conviction shall be adjudged to forfeit cloths so sold with costs of suits besides and moreover be still obliged to complete his engagements".

Regulation V: "Persons procuring from weavers in the Company's service, by the offer of ready money or on presence of previous engagements which are not avowed, cloths really wrought for the Company and with advances, knowing such cloths to be the right of the Company, either by the mark upon them or the transactions between the weavers from whom they procure them and the Company or having reasons for such knowledge from the notoriety of those weavers being in the Company's employ, shall on the proof of the fact in the Adalats, be subjects to such punishments as the nature of the offence may appear to deserve".

Regulation VI : "A list of register of the weavers employed by the Company in every Pergunnah with their places of abode, shall be stuck up by the Commercial Agents there, in the cutcherry of that Pergunnah".

Additional supplement to the Regulations for weavers 30th September, 1789.

Regulation XV: "Weavers possessed of more than one loom and entertaining one or more workmen, shall be subject to the following penalties on failing to deliver cloth at the stipulated period expressed in written agreement. To the Company for every piece of cloth not delivered according to the agreement,[35] per cent on the stipulated price of such cloth, besides the repayment of money advanced for the same."

Source : *Proceedings of Board of Trade (Commercial)* 3rd June, 1783, Proceeding No. 30, Vol. 37. Taken from D.B. Mitra, *The Cotton Weavers of Bengal* (1757-1833), Calcutta, 1978, pp. 222-25.

GLOSSARY

Amberty (Amriti)	:	Superior grade of white cloth.
Aurung	:	Place of manufacture.
Banian	:	Native merchant or tradesman.
Calico	:	A name used in European sources. The modern meaning is plain, white unprinted cotton cloth, bleached or unbleached.
Chadar	:	Wrapper or bed sheet.
Chautar	:	High priced cotton stuff.
Chini	:	Refined sugar.
Chintz	:	A type of cotton cloth (usually calico) with floral or other patterns printed or painted.
Cora	:	Unbleached state.
Coss	:	A measure of about 2 miles.
Cuttanee	:	A female spinner.
Dalal	:	Broker.
Dastak	:	Permit.
Dhutties	:	Calico, thick and strong enough for use as sail-cloth worn by male.
Diwan	:	Receiver-General of a Province.
Diwani	:	The office or jurisdiction of a Diwan.
Diwani Adalat	:	A court for trying revenue and other civil causes.
Farman	:	An imperial decree.
Faujdari Adalat	:	A court having charge of the police and with jurisdiction in all criminal matters.
Gazi (ganzzee)	:	Low priced cotton cloth; also coarse undergarments worn by male in the upper part of the body.
Golah	:	Godown.
Gomasta	:	An Indian Agent.
Karkhana	:	Workshop.

Kist	:	Instalment.
Koya	:	Cocoon (silk).
Malkana	:	Proprietor of soil/land.
Mulmul	:	A kind of muslin.
Muslin	:	Name used in European sources for light semi-transparent cotton cloth made of very fine yarn.
Russoom	:	a kind of illegal tax
Salami	:	a kind of tribute.
Nad	:	A type of earthen pot.
Naib	:	Deputy.
Patang (Guddi)	:	Kite.
Rai-raiyan	:	Chief of the Rai (An Indian noble man).
Sela (Shela)	:	High-priced cotton stuff, sometimes used for a coarse kind of muslin.
Ser	:	A measure of weight slightly less than a kilogram.
Shatranji	:	A high-priced woollen carpet woven in India. However, here used for carpet woven of cotton.
Shukkar	:	Sugar in crude form.
Sira	:	Liquid of boiled sugarcane.
Zillah	:	District.

BIBLIOGRAPHY

PRIMARY SOURCES

Unpublished

Guide to the Records in National Archives of India, Part II, Home Department/Ministry of Home Affairs (1748-1957), New Delhi, 1977.

Published

Abul Fazl, *Ain-i Akbari,* translated by H.S. Jarrett, Reprint, Delhi, 1978.

Ambasthya, B.P. (ed.), *Beams' Contribution to the Political Geography of Subah of Awadh, Bihar, Bengal and Orissa in the Age of Akbar*, Patna, Reprint, 1976.

Bains, Edward, *History of Cotton Manufacture in Great Britain,* London, 1837.

Banerjee, Anil Chandra, & Ghosh, Bimal Kanti (ed.) *: A Narrative of the Transactions in Bengal (1760-64)*, *Calcutta,* 1976.

Bolts, William, *Consideration on Indian Affairs,* London, 1772.

Buchanan, Francis, *An Account of the Districts of Bihar & Patna in 1811-12,* Patna, (not dated).

__ __, *An Account of the District of Purnea in 1809-10,* Purnea, 1939.

__ __, *An Account of the District of Bhagalpur, 1810-11,* Patna, 1928.

Datta, K.K. (ed.), *Fort William-India House Correspondence* Vol.I (1748-56), National Archives of India, Delhi, 1958.

__ __, *Catalogue of Patna Commissioner' Records* (1813-53), Patna, 1963.

Hasan, Syed Badrul, *Yadgar-e Rozgar,* Patna City, 1931.

Hunter, W.W., *Annals of Rural Bengal,* Calcutta, Reprint, 1965.

— —, *Statistical Account of Bengal*, Vol. XIV, Delhi, Reprint, 1976.

Jackson, V.H. (ed.), *Journal of Francis Buchanan Kept during the Survey of the Districts of Patna and Gaya in 1811-12*, edited with notes and introduction by V.H. Jackson.

Orme, R., *Historical Fragments of the Mughal Empire*, London, 1805.

Prasad, Bisheswar (ed.), *Fort William-India House Correspondence*, Vol. VI (1770-72) National Archives of India, Delhi, 1963.

Shah, Ali Mohammad, *Naqsh-e Paidar*, Patna City, 1924.

Sinha, H.N. (ed.), *Fort William-India House Correspondence*, Vol. II (1764-66), National Archives of India, Delhi, 1962.

Sinha, N.K. (ed.), *Fort William-India House Correspondence*, Vol. V (1767-69), National Archives of India, Delhi, 1959.

Srivasachari, C.S.(ed.), *Fort William-India House Correspondence, Vol. IV* (1764-66), National Archives of India, Delhi, 1962.

SECONDARY SOURCES

Ahmad,Qeyamuddin (ed.), *Patna Through the Ages: Glimpses of History, Society and Economy*, Patna, 1988.

Alam, Muzaffar, *The Crisis of Empire in Mughal North India : Awadh and the Punjab 1707-1748*, Delhi, 1986.

— —, 'Eastern India in the Early Eighteenth Century "Crisis" : Some Evidence from Bihar', *IESHR*, Vol. 28, no. 1, 1991, pp. 43-47.

Ali, M. Athar, *The Mughal Nobility Under Aurangzeb*, revised edn., Delhi, 1997, first published Aligarh, 1966.

— —, 'The Eighteenth Century : an Interpretation', *Indian Historical Review*, vol. 5, nos. 1-2, 1978-79, pp. 175-86.

— —, 'The Passing of Empire : The Mughal Case', *Modern Asian Studies*, vol. 9, no. 3, 1975, pp. 385-96.

Arasaratnam, S., 'Merchants and Commerce in Coromandel : Trends and Tendencies in the Eighteenth Century', in Leonard Blusse and Femme Gaastra (eds), *On the Eighteenth Century As a Category of Asian History : Van Leur in Retrospect, Aldershot*, 1998, pp. 261-88.

Arasaratnam, S., "Weavers, Merchants and Company", *IESHR*, XVII, No. 3, 1980.

Askari & Ahmad (ed.), *The Comprehensive History of Bihar*, Vol. II, Part II, Patna, 1976.

Bagchi, Amiya Kumar, "De-industrialization in Gangetic Bihar (1809-1901)", in *Essays in Honour of Professor S. C. Sarkar*, New Delhi, 1976.

Barnett, Richard B., *North India between Empire : Awadh, the Mughals, and the British, 1720-1801,* Berkeley, 1980.

Bayly, C.A., *Rulers, Townsmen and Bazaars : North India Society in the Age of British Expansion 1770-1870,* Cambridge, 1983, Indian edn, Delhi, 1992.

— —, and Sanjay Subrahmanyam, 'Portfolio Capitalists and the Political Economy of Early Modern India', *Indian Economic and social History Review,* vol. 25, no. 4, 1988, pp. 401-24.

Bhargava, Meena, 'Perception and Classification of the Rights of the Social Classes : Gorakhpur and the East India Company in the Late 18th and Early 19th centuries', *Indian Economic and Social History Review,* vol. 30, no. 2, 1993, pp. 215-37.

— —, *State, Society, and Ecology : Gorakhpur in Transition, 1750-1830,* Delhi, 1999.

Bhattacarya, S., 'Regional Economy 1757-1857—Eastern India', Dharma Kumar and Meghnad Desai (eds), *Cambridge Economic History of India, 1757-1970,* vol. II, Delhi, pp. 270-95.

Bhattacharya, S., *East India Co. & Economy of Bengal,* London, 1954.

Briggs, G.W., *The Chamars,* Delhi, 1920.

Calkins, P.B., 'The Formation of a Regionally Oriented Ruling Group in Bengal 1700-1740', *Journal of Asian Studies,* vol. no. 4, 1970, pp. 799-806.

Chandra, Satish, *Parties and Politics at the Mughal Court, 1707-1740,* Aligarh, 1959.

— —, Review of the Crisis of the Jagirdari System', in Satish Chandra, *Medieval India : Society, the Jagirdari Crisis, and the Village,* Delhi, 1982, pp. 61-75.

Chatterjee, N.L., "Anglo-Dutch Disputes in Bengal" in *PIHC*, 1939.

Chaudhuri K.N., The *Economic Development of India under the East India Company, 1814-1858,* Cambridge, 1971.

Chaudhuri, R., The *Evolution of Indian Industries,* Calcutta, 1939.

Chaudhury, Sushil, *From Prosperity to Decline : Eighteenth Century Bengal,* Delhi, 1995.

Chicherov, A.I., India. *Economic Development in the 16th-18th Centuries.* Outline History of Crafts & Trade, Moscow, 1971.

Cohn, Bernard S., 'The Initial British Impact on India : A Case Study of the Benares Region', in Bernard S. Cohn, *An Anthropologist among the Historians and Other Essays,* Delhi, 1987, pp. 320-42. (Essay first published in *Journal of Asian Studies,* vol. 19, no. 4, August 1960).

Das Gupta, Ashin, *Indian Merchants and the Decline of Surat : c. 1700-1750,* Weisbaden, 1979.

— —, 'Trade and Politics in 18th Century India', in D.S. Richards (ed.), *Islam and the Trade of Asia : A Colloquium,* Oxford, 1970, pp. 181-214.

Datta, K.K.(ed.), *The Comprehensive History of Bihar,* Vol.III, Part I, Patna, 1976.

— —, *Studies in the History of Bengal Subah,* Vol.I & II, Calcutta, 1936.

Datta, Rajat, 'Markets, Bullion and Bengal's Commercial Economy : an 18th Century Perspective', in Om Prakash and Denys Lombard (eds), *Commerce and Culture in the Bay of Bengal, 1500-1800,* Delhi, 1999, pp. 329-59.

— —, Society, *Economy and the Market : Commercialization in Rural Bengal c. 1760-1800,* Delhi, 2000.

Diwakar, R.R., *Bihar Through the Ages,* Calcutta, 1959.

Dutt, R.C., The *Economic History of India under the Early British Rule*, Vol. 1, (1757-1837), London, 1956.

Forbes, R.J., Studies *in Ancient Technology,* Vol. IV, Leiden, 1957.

Gadgil, D.R., *The Industrial Evolution of India in Recent Times,* Oxford University Press, 5th Edn. 1971.

Ghoshal, H.R., *Economic Transition in Bengal Presidency (1793-1833),* Patna, 1950.

Gopal, Surendra, *Patna in the 19th Century,* Calcutta, 1982.

Gordon, Stewart, *The Marathas, 1600-1818,* Cambridge, 1993.

— —, 'The Slow Conquest : Administrative Integrative of Malwa into the Maratha Empire 1720-60', *Modern Asian Studies,* vol. 11, no. 2, 1977, pp. 1-40.

— —, *Marathas, Marauders, and State Formation in Eighteenth Century India,* OUP, Delhi, 1994.

Guha, Sumit, 'Potentates, Traders and Peasants : Western India, c. 1700-1870', in Burton Stein and Sanjay Subrahmanyam (eds), *Institutions and Economic Change in South Asia,* Delhi, 1996, pp. 71-84.

Habib, Irfan, *An Atlas of the Mughal Empire*, OUP, 1982.

Habib, Irfan, *Essays in Indian History, Tulika* Publication, Delhi, 1995.

Habib, Irfan, *The Agrarian System of Mughal India, 1556-1705,* Delhi, 1963.

— —, 'Studying Colonial Economy without Colonialism', *Modern Asian Studies,* vol. 19, part 3, July 1985, pp. 355-81.

——, 'Processes of Accumulation inPre-colonial and Colonia India', *India Historical Review,* 1985-5, vol. xi, no. 1-2, July, 1984-5, pp. 65-90.

——, 'The 18th Century in Indian Economic History', *Proceedings of Indian History Congress,* 56th Session, Calcutta, 1995, pp. 358-78.

Kolff, D.H.A., *Naukar, Rajput, and Sepoy : The Ethnohistory of the Military Labour Market in Hindustan, 1450-1850,* Cambridge, 1990.

Krishnamurthy, J., 'Deindustrialization in Gangetic Bihar during the Nineteenth Century Another look at the evidence', *IESHR*, XXII, No. 4, 1985.

Kumar, Nita, *Artisans of Benaras: Popular-Culture and Identity,* Princeton, 1988.

Leonard, Karen, 'The Great Firm Theory of the Decline of Mughal Empire', *Comparative Studies in History and Society,* vol. 21, no. 2, 1979, pp. 161-67.

Marshall, P. J., *Bengal : The British Bridgehead, Eastern India 1740-1828,* Cambridge, 1987.

——, *East India Fortunes : The British in Bengal in the Eighteenth Century,* OXford, 1976.

Matsui, Toru, 'Towards a Re-interpretation of the 19th Century Indian Economic History', *IESHR, V,* No.l, 1968.

McLane, John R., *Land and Local Kingship in 18th Century Bengal,* Cambridge, 1993.

Menon, Dilip, 'Houses by the Sea : State Experimentation in Malabar 1760-1800', in Neera Chandoke (ed.), *Mapping History : Essays Presented to Ravinder Kumar,* Delhi, 2000, pp. 161-86.

Mishra, K.P., 'Textile Manufacture and the Company's Trade in late 18th Century North India, *PIHC,* (48th Session), Goa, 1988, pp.451-60.

Mitra, D.B., The *Cotton Weavers of Bengal* (1757-1833), Calcutta, 1978.

Morris, D. Morris, 'Towards a Re-interpretation of the Nineteenth Century Indian Economic History', *IESHR,*V, No. 1, 1968.

Mukherjee, R., 'Trade and Empire in Awadh, 1765-1804', *Past and Present,* no. 94, February 1982, pp. 84-102.

Naoroji, Dadabhai, *Poverty and un-British Rule in India,* London, 1901.

Naqvi, H.K., *Urban Centres & Industries in Upper India (1556-1803),* Calcutta, 1968.

Nightingal, Pamela, *Trade and Empire in Western India 1784-1806,* Cambridge, 1970.

Parthasarathi, Prasannan, 'Merchants and the Rise of Colonialism', in Burton Stein and Sanjay Subrahmanyam (eds), *Institutions and Economic Change in South Asia,* Delhi, 1996, pp. 85-104.

Pavlov, V.I., *Historical Premises for India's Transition to Capitalism,* Moscow, 1978.

Perlin, Frank, 'Of White Whale and Countrymen in 18th century Maratha Deccan', *Journal of Peasant Studies,* vol. 5, no. 2, 1978, pp. 172-237.

— —, 'State Formation Reconsidered', *Modern Asian Studies,* vol. 19, no, 3, 1985, pp. 415-80.

— —, 'Proto Industrialization and pre-colonial south Asia', *Past and Present,* no. 98, 1983, pp. 30-95.

Prakash, Om, 'Trade and Politics in Eighteenth-century Bengal', in Leonard Blusse and Femme Gaastra (eds), *On the Eighteenth Century as a Category of Asian History : Van Leur in Retropect,* Aldershot, 1998, pp. 237-60.

Raychouduri, Tapan and Habib Irfan, The *Cambridge Economic History of India,* Vol. I, Delhi, 1982.

Risley, H. H., *People of India,* 1908.

Singh, Dilbagh, *The Peasant and the State : Eastern Rajasthan in the 18th Century,* Delhi, 1990.

Singh, Chetan, *Region and Empire : Punjab in the Seventeenth Century,* Delhi, 1991.

Sing, Vipul, 'Professional Mobility and Change : The World of Artisans in Late Eighteenth Century Patna,' *Studies in History and Culture,* Vol. 4, No. 2, Sep. 1996, pp. 31-40.

Singh, Vipul, 'Pre-Industrial Technology : A Study of Craftsmanship in 18th Century Bihar', *Critique,* Vol. 2, No.1, Sep. 1998, pp.54-71.

Singh, Vipul, 'Professional Brotherhood and Change in Physical Environment : The Colonial Factor in, Administrative History of 18th Century Patna District', *The Geographer,* Vol. 47, No. 1, January 2000, pp. 70-85.

Sinha, N.K., *The Economic History of Bengal from Plassey to the Permanent Settlement,* Calcutta, 1965

Special Issue of Journal of Bihar & Orissa Research Society, on Buchanan's Report of Patna District, Patna, 1922.

Stein, Burton, 'State Formation and Economy Reconsidered', *Modern Asian Studies,* vol. 19, no. 3, July 1985, pp. 387-413.

Stokes, Eric, 'The First Century of British Colonial Rule : Social Revolution or Social Stagnation' in *Past and Present,* nos. 58-61, 1973, pp. 136-60. This also appears in Eric Stokes, *The Peasant and the Raj : Studies in Agrarian Society and Peasant Rebellion in Colonial India,* Cambridge, 1978, pp. 19-45.

Subramanian, Lakshmi, 'Power and the Weave : Weavers, Merchants and Rulers in Eighteenth-century Surat' in R. Mukherjee and L. Subramanian (eds), *Politics and Trade in The Indian Ocean World : Essays in Honour of Ashin Das Gupta,* Delhi, 1998, pp. 52-82.

Subrahmanyam, Sanjay, 'Institutions, Agency and Economic Change in south Asia : A Survey and Some Suggestions', in Burton Stein and Sanjay Subrahmanyam (eds), *Institutions and Economc Change in South Asia,* Delhi, 1996, pp. 14-47.

___, The Mughal State—Structure or Process? Reflections on Recent Western Historiography', *Indian Economic and Social History Review,* vol. 29, no. 3, 1992, pp. 291-321.

Sur, Nikhilt, 'The Bihar Famine of 1770', *IESHR,* XIII, No.4, 1976.

Thomas, P.J., 'The Indian Cotton Industry' in *Modern Review,* February, 1924.

Thorner, Daniel, 'De-industrialization in India, 1881-1931', *Land and Labour in India,* Bombay, 1965.

Washbrook, David, 'Land and Labour in Late Eighteenth—Century South India : The Golden Age of the Pariah?', in Peter Robb (ed.), *Dalit Movements and the Meanings of Labour in India,* Delhi, 1993, pp. 68-86.

Wink, Andre, *Land and Sovereignty in India : Agrarian Society and Politics under the Eighteenth-Century Maratha Svarajya,* Cambridge, 1986.

INDEX